SHIBA INU BIBLE AND SHIBA INUS
Your Perfect Shiba Inu Guide

Shiba Inu, Shiba Inus, Shiba Inu Puppies, Shiba Inu Breeders, Shiba Inu Care, Shiba Inu Training, Health, Behavior, Breeding, Grooming, History and More!

By Matthew Masterson

© DYM Worldwide Publishers, 2020.

Published by DYM Worldwide Publishers 2020.

ISBN: 978-1-913154-21-9

Copyright © DYM Worldwide Publishers, 2020
2 Lansdowne Row, Number 240 London W1J 6HL

ALL RIGHTS RESERVED. This book contains material protected under International & Federal Copyright Laws & Treaties. Any unauthorized reprint or use of this material is strictly prohibited. No part of this book may be reproduced or transmitted in any form or by any means, electronic, mechanical, or otherwise, including photocopying or recording, or by any information storage or retrieval system without the express written permission from the author.

Copyright and Trademarks. This publication is Copyright 2020 by DYM Worldwide Publishers. All products, publications, software, and services mentioned and recommended in this publication are protected by trademarks. In such an instance, all trademarks & copyright belonging to the respective owners.

All rights reserved. No part of this book may be reproduced or transferred in any form or by any means, graphic, electronic, or mechanical, including but not limited to photocopying, recording, taping, scanning, or by any information storage retrieval system, without the written permission of the author. Pictures used in this book are royalty-free pictures purchased from stock photo websites with full rights for use within this work.

Disclaimer and Legal Notice. This product is not legal or medical advice and should not be interpreted in that manner. You need to do your own due diligence to determine if the content of this product is right for you. The author, publisher, distributors, and or/affiliates of this product are not liable for any damages or losses associated with the content in this product. While every attempt has been made to verify the information shared in this publication, neither the author, publisher, distributors, and/or affiliates assume any responsibility for errors, omissions, or contrary interpretation of the subject matter herein. Any perceived slights to any specific person(s) or organization(s) are purely unintentional. We have no control over the nature, content, and availability of the websites listed in this book.

The inclusion of any website links does not necessarily imply a recommendation or endorse the views expressed within them. DYM Worldwide Publishers takes no responsibility for, and will not be liable for, the websites being temporarily or being removed from the Internet. The accuracy and completeness of the information provided herein and opinions stated herein are not guaranteed or warranted to produce any particular results, and the advice or strategies contained herein may not be suitable for every individual. The author, publisher, distributors, and/or affiliates shall not be liable for any loss incurred as a consequence of the use and application, directly or indirectly, of any information presented in this work. This publication is designed to provide information regarding the subject matter covered. The information included in this book has been compiled to give an overview of the topics covered. The information contained in this book has been compiled to provide an overview of the subject. It is not intended as medical advice and should not be construed as such. For a firm diagnosis of any medical conditions, you should consult a doctor or veterinarian (as related to animal health). The writer, publisher, distributors, and/or affiliates of this work are not responsible for any damages or negative consequences following any of the treatments or methods highlighted in this book.

Website links are for informational purposes only and should not be seen as a personal endorsement; the same applies to any products or services mentioned in this work. The reader should also be aware that although the web links included were correct at the time of writing, they may become out of date in the future. Any pricing or currency exchange rate information was accurate at the time of writing but may become out of date in the future. The Author, Publisher, distributors, and/or affiliates assume no responsibility for pricing and currency exchange rates mentioned within this work.

Table of Contents

Chapter 1 –   Introducing the Shiba Inu 11
Chapter 2 –   Shiba Inu History...15
              When Was the Shiba Inu Dog Developed? 15
              What Were Shiba Inus Bred to Do?..........................16
              Are Shiba Inu Japanese Dogs? 17
              What Does Shiba Inu Mean?....................................17
              Are Shibu Inu Dogs Popular Today?........................17
              Famous Shiba Inu 18
              Is the Shiba Inu Hypoallergenic?..............................19
              Shiba Inus in the United States 19
              The Shiba Inu in Canada...20
              The Shiba Inu in Japan..21

Chapter 3 – Shiba Inu Breed Standard 23
              What is the Shiba Inu Breed Standard?....................23
              Are There Different Types of Shiba Inu? 25
              What is the Ideal Shiba Dog Personality?.................26
              What is the Shiba Inu's Coat Like? 26
              What are the Accepted Colors for the
              Shiba Inu Coat?...26
              Is There Such a Thing as a Mini Shiba? 28
              What Should I Know About the Black Shiba?...........28
              What Should I Know About the Red Shiba Inu? 29
              What Should I Know About the Cream Shiba Inu?...30

What is a Mame Shiba Inu?..30
Is There Such a Thing as a White Shiba? 30

Chapter 4 – Is the Shiba the Right Dog for Me? 31
What is the Shiba Inu Temperament?.......................32
Is the Shiba Inu Aggressive? 32
Is the Shiba Inu Apartment-Friendly?.......................32
Will a Shiba Inu Puppy be a Good Addition
to My Family? 33
Is the Shiba Inu Good with Kids?...............................34
The Shiba Inu with Other Dogs—Will They
Get Along?...35
What is Shiba Inu Training Like? 36
I Am a Shiba Inu First Time Owner—What Do
I Need to Know?..37
What is the Average Shiba Inu Price? 37

Chapter 5 - Finding a Shiba Puppy 39
Where Can I Find Shiba Inu for Sale Near Me? 40
How Do I Find a Responsible Shiba Inu Breeder?.....40
What Should I Ask a Shiba Inu Breeder During
a Phone Interview? 41
What Should I Look for When I Visit a Shiba
Dog Breeder's Kennel? 42
How Do I Find a Shiba Inu Rescue Near Me?...........46

Chapter 6 – Puppy Mills 47
How Do I Know If I Am Dealing with a
Shiba Puppy Mill Breeder? 48
What Are Some Signs to Look for That May
Indicate I Am Contacting a Shiba Inu Puppy Mill?.....50
What Should I Know About Shiba Inu Pet
Store Puppies?..52

What Should I Know About Backyard Breeders? 53
A Final Word About Puppy Mills, Pet Store,
and Backyard Breeders 53

Chapter 7 – Getting Ready 55
How Do I Puppy-Proof My Home for My
Shiba Inu Puppy? 55
How Do I Introduce My Shiba Inu Puppy to My
Family and Other Pets? Shiba Inu and Cats—
Do They Get Along? 58
What Shiba Inu Supplies Do I Need?
Shiba Inu Gear 60

Chapter 8 – Shiba Inu Nutrition 65
What Are the Nutritional Requirements of
Shiba Inus? 66
What is the Best Shiba Inu Food? 66
How Much Should I Feed My Shiba Inu? 67
What Should I Feed My Older Shiba Inu? 68
How Are Diet and Health Connected in
Shiba Inus? 69
Is Dry Dog Food or Canned Dog Food Better
for My Shiba Inu? 70
What Should I Know About Raw Diets? 70
What Do I Need to Know About Making
Homemade Dog Food for My Shiba Inu? 72
What are the Best Shiba Inu Dog Treats? 73
What Foods are Dangerous to Shiba Inus? 73

Chapter 9 – Shiba Inu Training 75
What Should I Know About Shiba Inu Training? 75
How To House Train Your Shiba Inu Puppy 76
Training Shiba Inu for Basic Obedience…Sit,
Stay, and Come 78

How to Train to Correct Bad Behavior 80
How Do I Train My Shiba Inu to do Tricks?............82
Avoiding Aggression 82
Socialization—Why It is Important and
How to Do It 83
Biting—Why Dogs Do It and How to Avoid It........84
Positive Reinforcement Training 85
Clicker Training...85

Chapter 10 – Shiba Inu Health..87
How Do I Find a Veterinarian for
My Shiba Inu Puppy? 87
What Should I Know About Vaccines for
My Shiba Puppy? 88
Will My Shiba Inu Puppy Have His First
Vaccines While at the Breeder's Home? 89
What Are Common Diseases Affecting the
Shiba Dog Breed?..90
Hip and Elbow Dysplasia in Shiba Inus 90
Common Eye Problems and the Shiba Inu..............91
Von Willebrand's Disease in Shiba Inus..................92
Patellar Luxation in the Shiba Dog 92
Neuronal Ceroid Lipofuscinosis in the Shiba Inu 93
Allergies in the Shiba Inu 93

Chapter 11 – Shiba Grooming 95
Shiba Inu Grooming Tools..96
What Do I Need to Know About Shiba Inu
Bathing? Is There a Specific Shiba Inu Shampoo? 96
What Do I Need to Know About Shiba Inu
Toenail Care?...97

What Do I Need to Know About Shiba Inu
Dental Care? 99
What Do I Need to Know About Shiba Inu
Ear Care? 99

Chapter 12 – Showing a Shiba 101
What Do I Need to Know About the
AKC Shiba Inu? 102
Can Any Shiba Inu Be Shown at a Dog Show? 103
How Do I Select a Good Shiba Inu Puppy
to Compete in Dog Shows? 104
What Coat Colors are Accepted in the
AKC Shiba? 105
Are Shiba Inus Good for Dog Sports
Competitions and Agility Contests? 105

Chapter 13 – Working Shiba Inus 107
The Shiba Inu Therapy Dog 108
The Shiba Inu Police Dog 108
Shiba Inu Guard Dog 109

Chapter 14 – Breeding 111
How Do I Find a Mate for My Shiba Inu? 113
What is the Shiba Inu Heat Cycle? 114
What Should I Know About the Shiba Inu
Mating Process? 115
What Should I Know About Shiba Inu Pregnancy? 115
How Do I Help to Prepare My Shiba Inu
to Give Birth? 116
What Should I Know About Shiba Inu Labor
and Delivery? 118
How Do I Care for Newborn Shiba Inu Puppies? 118

Chapter 15 – Shiba Inu Mixes 121
    Husky Inu 121
    Shih Poms 122
    Shiba Retriever 123
    Corgi Inu 123
    Shepherd Inus 124

Chapter 16 – Senior Shiba Inus 127
    What Changes in Diet and Nutrition Will
    My Shiba Inu Experience? 128
    What Changes Will Occur in My Shiba Inu's
    Drinking Habits and Bowel and Bladder Functions?...129
    What Do I Need to Know About Joint Pain and
    Stiffness in the Shiba Inu? 130
    What Do I Need to Know About Vision and
    Hearing Problems in the Shiba Dog? 131
    What Do I Need to Know About Memory Loss
    and Confusion in Shiba Inus? 132
    What Do I Need to Know About Changing
    Personality and Disposition in Shiba Inus? 132

Chapter 17 - Conclusion 135

Bonus Chapter – Shiba Inu for Sale and Adoption 139
    Shiba Inu Breeders in the United States 139
    Shiba Inu Breeders in Canada 141
    Shiba Inu Breeders in the U.K. 142
    Shiba Inu Rescue Groups in the United States 142
    Shiba Inu Rescue Groups in Canada 143
    Shiba Inu Rescue Groups in the U.K. 143

CHAPTER 1

Introducing the Shiba Inu

The Shiba Inu is a unique breed believed to be of Japanese descent that traces its roots to the Asian Gray Wolf. The breed has changed very little over the years, remaining true to its appearance, working ability, and personality traits. Shibas are a breed known to be immensely loyal to their families while still retaining a strong tendency towards independence of thought and actions. While the breed is often characterized by its standoffish nature and quiet dignity, the Shiba is equally playful and fun-loving as well.

The Shiba Inu breed was originally developed to assist its owners on hunting expeditions in its native Japan. Artist renderings from 300 years ago depict the breed engaged in hunts for such game as deer, wild boar, and even bear. But the Shiba Inu was also a great help to hunters who favored the pursuit of small game animals such as squirrels, rabbits, and raccoons.

An extremely versatile dog breed, the Shiba Inu easily fulfilled many different roles as a working dog. In addition to the Shiba's skills as a loyal hunting companion, this dog breed has also enjoyed work as a guard dog protecting its master's home and hearth, a fighting dog, and, most importantly, a beloved family pet.

When the mixing of breeds became common, a sincere effort was made by Saito Hirokichi in 1928 to protect and preserve the heritage of the Shiba Inu. His efforts were richly rewarded when, in 1932, the country declared the Shiba Inu a "national treasure."

During World War II, when the Shiba Inu was no longer required to fulfill its previous working roles, the breed was in danger of disappearing from the landscape entirely. Great efforts were undertaken to ensure the breed's secured future as a much-loved working dog and family companion.

The Shiba Inu temperament is characterized by its bold, fearless spirit, which is always well balanced by its excellent nature. A dog highly prized for its independence, the Shiba approaches strangers with caution but bonds deeply to its family with whom it is quite affectionate. Shibas are wary by nature, meaning it takes time to build a relationship of trust and respect.

The Shiba Inu is known for its extreme loyalty to its family. But Shibas have a playful side too!

The Shiba Inu can be prone to aggression towards other dogs, but this trait should never be exhibited towards people. Early socialization with other dogs who have displayed proper canine manners, is the best way to prevent any potential canine aggression from developing. Though considered a small dog, Shibas are immensely confident and lack the ability to recognize their own size, believing they have the physical stature to back up their attitude. This can lead to conflict with other dogs if care is not taken to properly supervise all canine interactions.

Shiba Inus should also be very carefully introduced to children. Though they are quite patient in general, they will retreat into their own space when they become uncomfortable; a practice that should be valued and rewarded. Forcing a Shiba to remain in a situation that is causing them discomfort could lead to the dog snapping out of frustration. It is important that all interactions between a child and a dog be supervised for the safety of both parties involved.

This guidebook to the Shiba Inu is intended to provide valuable insights into the breed and its unique characteristics. From information on proper care and feeding of the Shiba Inu to training and how to find a reputable breeder, you will find everything you need in this one in-depth volume.

The Shiba Inu is an old and well loved breed with much to offer. For an affectionate, loyal family companion with the intelligence and independence to keep you on your toes, you can't go wrong by adding one of these lovable characters to your home!

CHAPTER 2
Shiba Inu History

The Shiba Inu is an ancient breed developed in Japan. A direct descendant of the Asian Gray Wolf, the original prototype of the Shiba Inu, was refined into six different breeds who expressed physical variations according to their geographical locations. Many of these six new breed types bore similarities with one main difference: size. Of the six, the Shiba Inu is the smallest.

When Was the Shiba Inu Dog Developed?

The Shiba is believed to trace its roots back to 300 B.C. In all of this time, the breed has undergone very few changes and essentially remains the same in temperament, conformation, and working ability. Though the Shiba Inu is no longer used as a fighting dog, the breed is still highly valued as a hunter and guard dog.

The Shiba Inu is one of few dog breeds that can trace its roots back to one animal: the Asian Gray Wolf. Recent DNA studies show that there are few genetic variations between the wolf and the domesticated Shiba Inu that is a much-loved family companion today. While most purebred breeds of today endured a long period of development during which time several breeds were combined to create a new hybrid, the Shiba Inu is the result of selective breeding of the Asian Gray Wolf alone.

What Were Shiba Inus Bred to Do?

The Shiba Inu was originally developed to serve as an avid hunting companion for its owners. A dog breed known for its confidence and depth of courage, the Shiba Inu, was employed in hunting both large and small game animals, including bear, wild boar, deer, squirrels, raccoons, and rabbits. Due to its penchant for boldness, Shiba Inus were often selected to participate in dogfighting rings, a practice that is now illegal.

The Shiba Inu is also highly prized for its bold, brave nature, making it well-suited to work as a guard dog. Since the Shiba is a tremendously loyal dog breed, it is only too happy to provide oversight and protection for its master's home and hearth.

Though playful by nature, the Shiba Inu was also a highly valued working dog whose roles included hunting, fighting, and guarding property.

Are Shiba Inu Japanese Dogs?

The Shiba Inu originated in Japan and enjoyed many years there as a beloved family companion and working dog. In 1928, the breed became in danger of extinction, and great efforts were undertaken to preserve this important dog breed for generations to come. These attempts were largely successful with the Shiba Inu dog being declared a "national treasure" in 1932.

Following World War II, the Shiba Inu population was greatly impacted by a prevalence of distemper, which decimated the dog community at large. The war-torn economy also made keeping a dog as a companion animal an undue financial hardship for many. A group called Nihonken Hozonkai (Nippo) was established with the intent of assisting local breeders to maintain viable breeding operations to continue the preservation of the beloved Shiba Inu.

What Does Shiba Inu Mean?

The name Shiba Inu is taken from two separate Japanese words. Legend states that "Shiba" means brushwood and was bestowed upon the dog breed due to the terrain the dog regularly traversed when out on a hunt. Equally possible is the belief that Shiba refers to the breed's most commonly seen color, an intense and attractive reddish hue. "Inu" is fair easier to explain. It is a Japanese word that simply translates to dog.

Are Shibu Inu Dogs Popular Today?

The Shiba Inu is a less common dog breed when compared with more frequently seen family companion animals such as the Golden Retriever, the Poodle, or the Australian Shepherd.

However, this cherished working breed still takes pride of place in the homes of many families today.

The Shiba Inu was declared a "national treasure" in 1932.

Famous Shiba Inu

Though Shiba Inu dogs are not as commonly seen in pop culture today, there are several who have attained their own unique following. One of the most famous Shiba Inus is a male dog named Marutaro. A 9-year-old dog, Marutaro quickly reached Instagram fame and reached as many as 2.4 million followers on the photo-sharing site. Through his handsome good looks and fluffy coat alone, Marutaro was Japan's second most well-known celebrity and he earned the same number of Instagram fans as famed skateboarder Tony Hawk.

Marutaro, also referred to simply as Maru, is the star of many different commercials and photo exhibits. In addition to his celebrity lifestyle as an actor and model, Maru has also been featured on the cover of Vogue Girl magazine and has his own shop in Japan.

Maru rose to fame following the tragic Japan earthquake and tsunami in 2011. His owner began posting photos of him to help provide comfort and encouragement to those suffering the after-effects of the destruction.

Another Shiba Inu dog who has achieved celebrity status is a little girl by the name of Mari. Mari and her owner make comedic videos based on interesting storylines where the duo recreates scenes worthy of the best Laurel and Hardy sketches. Today, there are over 100 of these videos posted on Youtube for people to enjoy, and there is even a DVD featuring fan favorites that can be purchased by those who can't get enough of this adorable team.

Is the Shiba Inu Hypoallergenic?

The Shiba Inu dog, like many breeds designed to work in inclement weather conditions, is in possession of a thick double coat. This coat does shed regularly and is prone to trapping dander. As such, the breed cannot be considered hypoallergenic.

For families suffering from allergies, it is important to note that the Shiba Inu will blow its coat twice early, a process that leads to intense shedding throughout the home.

Shiba Inus in the United States

The Shiba Inu dog was first brought to the United States in 1954, making its history in America relatively young. Over the years, the breed has increased in popularity in the United States. The Shiba first achieved recognition with the American Kennel Club (AKC) in the Non-Sporting Group in June of 1993.

The Shiba Inu in Canada

Shiba Inus were introduced to Canada through Japanese immigrants who moved to the area, bringing their beloved dogs with them. In the early 1980s, several Shibas who were bred in the United States were imported to Canada, and small breeding programs were born in the country.

To advance the breed towards the Canadian Kennel Club (CKC) recognition, a group of breeders established a national breed club. In 1992, an application was submitted to the CKC requesting consideration for breed status within the esteemed organization. A breed standard was developed from the original standard outlined by Nippo. In January of 2006, the Shiba Inu was granted full recognition with the CKC.

The Shiba Inu is now a recognized breed in both Canada and the United States. In his native Japan, he is the #1 choice for a companion dog.

The Shiba Inu in Japan

Today, the Shiba Inu is the number one companion dog in its native Japan. Though rarely used for hunting anymore, the Shiba Inu dog remains a beloved family pet.

CHAPTER 3
Shiba Inu Breed Standard

Shiba Inus are a breed that is small in size but big on personality. An alert, active family companion, the Shiba is characterized by its natural aloofness coupled with its good-natured ways. A dog breed developed to traverse mountainous terrain, the Shiba Inu is a strong dog with excellent stamina. Courageous, bold, and extremely loyal, the Shiba Inu is easy to love. The Shiba traces its roots directly back to the Asian Gray Wolf and is one of the world's oldest dog breeds.

What is the Shiba Inu Breed Standard?

The Shiba Inu breed standard defines the hallmarks by which the breed can be identified. It outlines the ideal characteristics each dog should display and is the "standard" all reputable breeders uphold as the "Bible" to emulate.

The standard for the Shiba Inu dog states that the breed is the smallest of the dog types tracing their roots to Japan. Since the breed was developed with the intent of hunting at night and through the use of scent, the ideal Shiba should be alert, agile of body, and in possession of very acute senses.

According to the standard, the Shiba Inu should be well-muscled to properly support its role as a working dog. Males should range in height from 14.5" to 16.5" (37-42 cm) at the shoulder, with females slightly shorter at 13.5" to 15.5" (34-39 cm). Males should look distinctly masculine, while females should be uniquely feminine in appearance. It is preferred that the Shiba Inu be of moderate size, aiming for the middle of the height range and not the extremes found on either end.

The Shiba Inu's preferred weight is 23 pounds (10 kg) for male dogs and 17 pounds (8 kg) for females.

The ideal Shiba head displays a friendly expression that communicates confidence. The eye shape is triangular with the eyes deep brown in hue, and the lids rimmed in black. The ears are small in size, triangular in shape, and stand at attention at the top of the head. This ear type is commonly referred to as "prick ears." The ears should be in balance with the head and size of the body.

One of the defining characteristics of the breed is the tail, which can be sickle-shaped or double curled.

Shiba Inus usually range from 17 to 23 pounds (8 to 10 kg.) in weight.

Are There Different Types of Shiba Inu?

Though some breeds do come in several different size variations, these do not exist in the Shiba Inu. The Shiba is considered a small breed dog and does not come in miniature or giant versions.

What is the Ideal Shiba Dog Personality?

The Shiba Inu is a friendly dog with its family but is a dog that maintains a reservedness for strangers. It takes time and patience to earn the Shiba's trust, but once it is established, loyalty and affection soon follow.

The breed is well-renowned for its bold, confident nature. Shiba Inu dogs are naturally fiercely independent, a quality that serves them well as hunting companions for their beloved owners.

What is the Shiba Inu's Coat Like?

The Shiba Inu has a thick double coat, which is comprised of a topcoat and an undercoat. The topcoat is stiff to the touch and should be completely straight and short throughout the body. The undercoat is much softer and thicker. On the outer portion of the topcoat are guard hairs. The purpose of the guard hairs is to provide additional protection for the coat during inclement weather conditions. The guard hairs typically stand away from the body of the coat and can measure 1" to 2" in length.

The tail is the one area of the body where the hair is marginally longer. It should be displayed in a brush-like pattern.

What are the Accepted Colors for the Shiba Inu Coat?

There are four accepted colors for the Shiba Inu coat. They are as follows:

- Black and tan
- Cream

- Red
- Red sesame (red with black points)

The breed standard states that regardless of coat color, each of the dominant shades should be vibrant. The undercoat comes in three different color variations: cream, buff, or gray.

A defining characteristic of the Shiba's coat is something known as Urajiro. Urajiro is essentially a color for markings which can range from cream to white, and they must be displayed on the following areas of the Shiba Inu regardless of the base coat color:

- Sides of the muzzle
- On the cheeks
- Inside the ears
- Underneath the jaw
- On the inside of the legs
- On the abdomen
- Around the anus region
- Around the area where the tail connects to the anus

Each color variation also has its own detailed set of markings. Red dogs should have Urajiro markings located on the throat, forechest, and chest. Black and tans and red sesames often have a mark in the shape of a triangle on each side of the forechest.

Shiba Inus come in several different coat colors.

Is There Such a Thing as a Mini Shiba?

No, there is no such thing as a Miniature Shiba Inu. Breeders who claim to have this size variant of the breed available achieve the result by breeding undersized Shiba Inus together to produce puppies, which typically will not meet the size requirements specified in the standard. This practice is highly frowned upon as it can lead to serious health complications in future generations.

What Should I Know About the Black Shiba?

The black and tan Shiba Inu is actually a tri-colored coat given that Urajiro markings are present in addition to the tan points found throughout the body. The base of the coat is solid black.

As with all color types in the Shiba Inu dog, the black and tan coat should remain vibrant in hue. The black hair should have a sheen to it as well as a faint bronze tinge in the light. The undercoat of a black and tan Shiba should be buff or gray in color.

The markings should ideally be found between patches of black and white, preferably restricted to eye spots, cheeks, inside the ears, the legs, and the tail.

The Urajiro markings remain consistent through all four accepted colors. However, in the black and tan Shiba, the placement of the Urajiro gives the illusion of a white bow tie.

What Should I Know About the Red Shiba Inu?

The red coat is by far the most popular color for the Shiba Inu. Traditionally, it is the coat

color most commonly associated with the breed. Red is the dominant color genetically; hence, why it is the coat color, which is most typically seen in Shiba Inus.

The overall red coat is an excellent canvas from which to view the structure and detail of the Urajiro on the Shiba Inu's body. Other coat colors provide a backdrop that makes the unique markings more challenging to discern, particularly cream coats.

The standard states that the topcoat of the red Shiba Inu dog should be rich and distinct with a gray undercoat.

Red sesames (red with black points) are extremely rare. The most important component of a red sesame coat is that the black tipping is evenly distributed throughout the coat and not clumped into distinctive patches of color. Since this is very difficult to achieve, most reputable breeders do not make the attaining of red sesame coats a priority of their breeding program.

What Should I Know About the Cream Shiba Inu?

While cream is an accepted color for the Shiba Inu, it is not as popular as the dog's base color makes it difficult to see its unique and required Urajiro markings.

What is a Mame Shiba Inu?

A Mame Shiba Inu is essentially a miniature Shiba. These dogs have been bred solely with the purpose of creating puppies that will grow up to be much smaller than the standard prescribes. This is a moneymaking scheme with little regard for the future health of the puppies.

Breeders of Mame Shiba Inus should be avoided.

Is There Such a Thing as a White Shiba?

No. White is not an accepted color for Shiba Inus.

CHAPTER 4

Is the Shiba the Right Dog for Me?

I f you are looking for a dog breed with a spirit of independence and the drive to keep up with your active lifestyle, the Shiba Inu just might be the perfect dog for you. A dog breed that is loyal to its core when it comes to its family, you will gain the best of both worlds with the Shiba Inu: a loyal family companion that loves to work and to play. Affectionate with its people, the Shiba loves nothing more than to cuddle up on the couch with its family when the day is done.

The Shiba Inu is fun-loving, loyal, and affectionate with its family.

What is the Shiba Inu Temperament?

The Shiba Inu is a bold, friendly, confident little dog. A breed known for its loyalty and courage, the Shiba will not back down from a challenge but does not actively seek out opportunities for conflict.

A breed that is playful and exceptionally good-natured, the Shiba is extremely affectionate with its family members but wary and aloof with strangers. If time and effort are invested in building a relationship with the dog, strangers will find the Shiba soon changes from reserved to loving and attention-seeking once trust has been established.

Is the Shiba Inu Aggressive?

The Shiba Inu should never be aggressive with people. However, dog aggression has been documented in the breed. To prevent this from becoming a problem, it is important to socialize the Shiba early with other socially appropriate dogs. All dog to dog interactions should be carefully supervised for the safety of both pets.

Is the Shiba Inu Apartment-Friendly?

Though the Shiba Inu was bred to be a working dog with the stamina to easily traverse vast tracts of mountainous terrain, it does not require extensive bouts of exercise each day to remain healthy and content. The Shiba is considered a small dog breed, and thus, can adapt well to apartment living. However, regular daily exercise is important to maintain a proper body condition and excellent health, so it is important to ensure the Shiba Inu is walked frequently.

Will a Shiba Inu Puppy be a Good Addition to My Family?

The Shiba Inu is a wonderful dog breed; however, it is not the right dog for every family. Shiba Inus bond deeply to their families and are known to be both affectionate and loyal. While they are known to be tolerant with children, they will avoid excess foolish behavior and will choose to withdraw from family life when play becomes too rowdy.

Families with children should take exceptional care to teach their kids the appropriate way to play with and handle their Shiba Inu puppy. All interactions with the dog and the child should be carefully supervised with play interrupted if it becomes too rough, or the dog is expressing discomfort.

The Shiba Inu requires only a moderate amount of daily exercise, making it a good choice for families who enjoy spending time outdoors, but that only have a limited amount of time to spend exercising their dog.

The Shiba Inu is a friendly, confident dog, but it is naturally wary of strangers. If your home is a revolving door of guests, this could prove challenging for your Shiba Inu puppy.

If your goals for a puppy include a playful, affectionate family companion, the Shiba Inu might be the right dog for you!

Is the Shiba Inu Good with Kids?

Shiba Inus are patient with children; however, they are not a dog breed that enjoys foolish or rough play. When this occurs, the Shiba will choose to withdraw to avoid confrontation.

Since Shiba Inus are instinctively protective with their family members, they will naturally watch over the youngest members of their family to keep them safe. They are also playful and affectionate, making them a good choice for families with children with one important caveat: all interactions between a Shiba Inu and children should be carefully supervised. Children should also be taught how to properly handle and play with a dog to prevent any conflicts from arising. Establishing boundaries early and teaching children to respect a dog and its comfort zone will go a long way to creating a happy bond between a Shiba Inu and its youngest family members.

Shiba Inus are patient with children, but all interactions with dogs are kids should be carefully supervised as a precaution.

The Shiba Inu with Other Dogs—Will They Get Along?

Shiba Inus can be prone to dog on dog aggression. Because this is a natural breed trait, it is best to introduce a Shiba Inu into a home with other dogs while it is still a puppy. Introducing a puppy into an established family is much safer since the other dogs in the home do not view the puppy as a threat to their hierarchy in the home.

But perhaps even more significant than this is the fact that a Shiba Inu puppy is still learning how to interact with other members of its own species. If a Shiba is introduced to other safe members of a canine family at a young age, chances are far greater that the pup will learn to get along well with other dogs. This, however, is not a guarantee that the Shiba will respond in kind to dogs outside its home, but it is a good way to set the puppy up for success. Early socialization with dogs proven to be of excellent temperament and in possession of good canine manners is key to helping a Shiba Inu learn the proper way to make and maintain canine friends.

In some cases, it is not possible for a Shiba Inu to get along with the resident dogs. In these situations, it will be necessary to crate and rotate the dogs, so they are each allowed separate time with their family or to rehome one of the dogs to allow for the best possible quality of life.

What is Shiba Inu Training Like?

Since Shiba Inus are independent thinkers, it is far easier to train them using positive reinforcement training techniques. All Shibas should be taught basic obedience commands such as sit, stay, come, and down, as these vital skills have the ability to save your dog's life in an emergency situation.

Shibas are extremely smart, but their desire for independence makes them a challenge to train. The best approach to learning new things is to use delicious treats to encourage your Shiba to cooperate during training sessions. The wise Shiba owner makes use of shaping exercises to encourage the dog to offer the behavior they are seeking then richly rewarding it with treats and praise when the dog willingly complies. Creating a training atmosphere that allows the dog to think the newly acquired skill was their idea in the first place is a key to helping your dog learn.

It is recommended that all Shiba Inu puppies participate in a puppy socialization class. Once that training has been successfully completed, basic obedience can begin.

I Am a Shiba Inu First Time Owner—What Do I Need to Know?

The Shiba Inu is not typically a difficult dog breed for the first-time owner to handle. However, it is always a good idea for families to understand traits that are specific to their breed of choice. This knowledge can then set them up for success in future training efforts and activities they will engage in together.

Perhaps the two most important things new Shiba Inu owners need to know is that the Shiba can be prone to dog aggression and that the breed is naturally wary of strangers. Because of these two things, it is vitally important that first-time owners not force the dog to engage with people or dogs if the Shiba is exhibiting signs that it is ill at ease.

What is the Average Shiba Inu Price?

Since there is no standardized pricing for Shiba Inus, prices vary according to popularity of the breed within that region, whether you wish to purchase a pet or a show quality puppy, and more. In conducting your research, it is best to avoid extremes in prices. It is true that you do get what you pay for. If the price seems too good to be true, it most likely is. Paying a low price for a puppy now may equate to paying much higher veterinary bills for a sick dog later. Likewise, prices that are far above the standard average or that are based on unusual things such as color or gender should be avoided.

As a basic average, you can expect to pay between $1,400-$2,200 USD (1,085-1,705 GBP) for a pet puppy from a reputable breeder. Show quality puppies start at $2,000 (1,550 GBP) and can range as high as $3,500 USD (2,710 GBP).

CHAPTER 5

Finding a Shiba Puppy

If you have decided that the Shiba Inu is the right breed for you, it is now time to begin the search for the breeder from which to purchase your new Shiba Inu family member.

It is important to carefully research reputable Shiba Inu breeders to find the right puppy for your family.

Where Can I Find Shiba Inu for Sale Near Me?

Any search for a Shiba Inu puppy or adult dog should first begin with breeder listings on such reputable organizations as the AKC Marketplace. These online portals keep a database of AKC registered breeders across the country. The breeder profiles are frequently updated to reflect current litters, available puppies, and prices. Contact information is provided for each breeder, allowing you the opportunity to contact the person yourself for more in-depth information.

How Do I Find a Responsible Shiba Inu Breeder?

In today's online world, it is quite easy for people to list puppies or adult dogs for sale on the Internet or in online editions of the newspaper. Reputable breeders usually have waiting lists for their puppies which can stretch from months to years or longer. They have no need to advertise on online marketplaces or in the paper as their puppies are most typically spoken for long before they are born.

A great resource to assist you with your search for your Shiba Inu puppy is your veterinarian. Your vet comes in contact with many different breeds on a daily basis and will likely be able to point you in the right direction when it comes to reputable Shiba Inu dog breeders.

Most breeds also have their own national clubs which help to connect puppy seekers with reputable breeders. This can also be an invaluable tool both in your breed research and in sourcing a Shiba Inu puppy that is closest to where you live. Most national breed club websites are heavy on education and list such important details as recommended health testing for breeding dogs and training advice for first-time owners of the breed.

If you have any friends who happen to own Shiba Inus, they too can help you in your search for your ideal Shiba puppy.

What Should I Ask a Shiba Inu Breeder During a Phone Interview?

Most of the initial contact with a Shiba Inu breeder will come via the phone or an internet inquiry. When you call or e-mail the breeder, it will be important for you to have a list of questions on hand for you to ask. During this first conversation, you will want to glean as much information as you can from the breeder to try to understand their expectations as well as their breeding and rearing practices.

Reputable breeders do not mind being asked questions. In fact, they welcome them! If you purchase a puppy from this person, you will be connected to them for the life of the dog. It is important to understand ahead of time what you are committing to and what will be expected of you over the course of the life of your Shiba Inu pup.

Among the questions you should ask are:

- What are the common genetic diseases for the Shiba Inu? Have both parents been tested for them?
- May I see the health test reports for both parents?
- At what age are the puppies ready to leave for their new homes?
- What is your process for puppy socialization? Have the puppies been socialized with children? Have they met other dogs?
- May I meet the puppies' parents?
- Do you offer a health guarantee? What does it include?

- What vaccination schedule do you recommend?
- What type of food do you feed your puppies and adult dogs?
- Do you have a contract I must sign? What requirements do you have of your puppy owners?
- What recommendations do you have for a first-time Shiba Inu owner?

Though this may seem like a lot of questions to ask someone you have just met, it is important to remember that the breeder will want to interview you as much as you want to interview them. A reputable breeder is looking for the ideal fit for their puppy. Getting to know you is a part of the process of determining if you are well-suited to the breed.

During the screening process, it may become evident to you that the breeder is simply not a good fit for you. This can occur for many different reasons. It is always best to go with your gut feeling. If something doesn't feel right, it is wise to move on to connecting with another breeder.

What Should I Look for When I Visit a Shiba Dog Breeder's Kennel?

From your phone call or email interactions, you should be able to narrow down your list of breeders to one or two who are worthy of more serious consideration. Once you have a "short list" of Shiba Inu breeders you feel comfortable with, it is time to request an appointment to visit their homes.

A visit to a breeder's kennel is an important step in the puppy selection process. Since puppies learn the most they will ever learn in their lifetime from birth to 16 weeks of age, those formative weeks in the breeder's home can make or break your puppy. You need to understand how your puppy was raised, what he or she has been exposed to, and what the environment is like that he or she lived in from the time of birth.

Most breeders expect potential puppy buyers will want to visit their homes to meet the puppies as well as the parents of the litter. When you visit a breeder's home, you both have the opportunity to get a glimpse into each other's lives and to establish if you are a good fit for each other.

Here are some things that you should watch carefully for during a visit to a breeder's kennel:

- **How the dogs live:**

    It is important for you to have the opportunity to see the area of the home where the puppies and adult dogs sleep and play. You should also ask to see the room where your future puppy was born if possible. This information is vital to understanding what your puppy has seen and experienced since the time of birth.

    One of the most important things you should see in the area where the dogs are living is signs of obvious care which includes clean and comfortable bedding, nutritious, high quality food, and easy access to clean drinking water. Should the home and/or kennel areas be lacking these essentials or dirty, this is not the breeder for you. Cleanliness is a non-negotiable must.

- **The health and temperament of the puppies:**

    When you visit the breeder's home, the breeder will most often allow you to see the entire litter of puppies, including any they plan to keep for themselves. This allows you to see the differences in personality and to observe each pup interacting with its littermates.

When you view the puppies, you want to see evidence that the pups are curious about their surroundings and show obvious signs of contentment and good health. Take note of any puppies who appear lethargic or who are showing signs of sickness or distress.

- **The health and temperament of the mother:**

   The temperament of the puppies' mother gives you a glimpse into what you can likely expect from your puppy in the future. A reputable breeder is proud of the parents of their puppies and will happily allow you to view the mother of the pups interacting with her babies.

   Mothers caring for their young should be of sufficient age and health to have whelped and reared a litter. This age is most typically two years old as the bitch is then physically and emotionally mature enough to care for a litter of her own.

   Mother dogs should be of excellent temperament and should be comfortable and content around their puppies. However, do not expect the mother to be in perfect coat condition. Hormones do wreak havoc with a mother dog's coat as do her puppies' sharp little nails and teeth. She should be clean, of excellent temperament, and in obvious good health.

How the mother is cared for should be of great concern to you. Reputable breeders cherish the mothers of their puppies and treat them well. If the puppies live like royalty while their mother is banished to dungeon like conditions, run! You may have stumbled upon a puppy mill.

Always ask to view the parents during a visit to a breeder. They give you a glimpse into what your puppy might be like when fully grown.

Be wary of any breeder who seems to rush you through the visit or who refuses you access to the mother or puppies. If the breeder steers you away from certain areas of the home where dogs are kept, it is also a cause for concern.

Another important red flag to consider is any breeder whose primary interest is money. If you feel pressured by the breeder to make a commitment to a sale on the spot, it is best that you move on to a different breeder. Reputable breeders understand that purchasing a puppy is a large commitment and should not be undertaken lightly. A visit to a kennel is one of several steps before agreeing to bringing a puppy home. Since reputable breeders are searching for forever homes for their puppies, they want to be as sure about you as you are about them. For this reason, they don't mind if you take your time thinking things over.

As a final consideration, the breeder's response to when the puppies are ready for their new homes will make or break whether or not this is the breeder for you. Under no circumstances should a puppy leave its mother before eight weeks of age. Those first eight weeks of a puppy's life are critical developmental periods when the mother dog teaches her puppies how to successfully navigate life as a dog in a human's world. If this time is missed, the knowledge lost cannot be replicated in any other way. While it is perfectly fine for a breeder to keep puppies for longer than eight weeks, letting them go sooner than that is harmful to the puppies and can lead to potential problems down the road.

During this visit, you should also discuss with the breeder what details are contained in their contract and what is expected of you as well as what you can expect for support in return. Many puppy contracts are negotiable, so if there are aspects within it that you would like amended, now is the time to discuss it.

How Do I Find a Shiba Inu Rescue Near Me?

If you've got your heart set on a Shiba Inu but are thinking a rescue might be the right dog for you, you will want to find out if there are any Shiba rescues in the near vicinity of your residence. A quick online search of local shelters will help identify if there are any dogs in your immediate area that might meet your desired criteria for your new family member.

Since Shiba Inu dogs are a rarer breed, you will most often have to consult online resources such as Petfinder to find Shibas that are up for adoption. National breed clubs can also assist as they are often aware of Shiba Inu dogs in need of rehoming.

CHAPTER 6

Puppy Mills

In your search for your new Shiba Inu puppy, you will want to take great care to avoid puppy mills. Puppy mills exist for one reason only: to mass produce puppies for pure profit. Since maximizing the amount of money they make per puppy is this type of breeder's main goal, they house their adult dogs and puppies in extremely poor living conditions. Little to no regard is given to the health and well-being of any of the animals in their care, leading to serious injury and illness which is left untreated. Most of the animals they own have never seen a vet or even stepped on grass or known the pleasure of playing with a toy.

Puppy mill operations have no regard for preserving a breed or ensuring the health and nutrition of the animals they own. They do not perform proper health testing to prevent passing on preventable, genetic illness, and most often do not vaccinate any of the animals in their care, meaning they are susceptible to serious and life-threatening diseases.

Supporting a puppy mill breeder through the purchase of a puppy feeds the cycle and encourages them to continue with their operations. Unfortunately, the dogs and puppies they produce are the true victims.

How Do I Know If I Am Dealing with a Shiba Puppy Mill Breeder?

There are many signs that can help you determine if the breeder you are considering owns and operates a puppy mill. It is important to familiarize yourself with these common characteristics to avoid purchasing a puppy from this type of operation.

Among the things you should look for are:

- The breeder has many different breeds of dogs available including several types of purebreds, hybrids, and designer dogs.
- The breeder has puppies available for sale all the time.
- The puppies are permitted to go to their new homes younger than eight weeks of age.
- The breeder refuses to permit a visit to their kennel.
- The breeder has no screening process for potential owners.
- The puppies are available for unusually low prices for that particular breed.
- The breeder offers no health guarantee.
- The breeder offers no support and provides no follow-up contact information.
- The puppies are not vaccinated or dewormed prior to leaving for their new homes.

Beware of the tell tall signs of a puppy mill breeder in your search for your Shibu Inu puppy.

All of these signs are red flags that you are dealing with a puppy mill breeder. Though there is nothing wrong with making a profit from breeding a litter, it should not be the primary focus of any reputable person's breeding program. Puppy mill breeders house their dogs in inhumane living conditions with many of them relegated to living in their own filth in cages far too small to even turn around in. Before making a commitment to purchase a puppy from any breeder, it is always wise to make a visit to the breeder's home to meet them as well as to have the opportunity to view the parents and the living conditions of the breeder's adult dogs and puppies.

Puppy mill puppies are also often not socialized. Since the first 16 weeks of a puppy's life mark the most formative developmental period, failure to introduce a pup to as many safe, novel experiences as possible during this time leaves the puppy at a serious disadvantage. As a result, the pup may grow up into a socially maladjusted pup who reacts to new situations with fear and aggression instead of curiosity and confidence.

What Are Some Signs to Look for That May Indicate I Am Contacting a Shiba Inu Puppy Mill?

Puppy mills continue to thrive because the public at large is often uninformed when it comes to what a reputable breeding facility looks like. When most people begin the search for a new puppy, they are excited and hoping that they can bring their new addition home soon, leading to impulse buys when presented with an adorable puppy that is ready to go home NOW.

Since the purchase of a purebred Shiba Inu puppy is an expensive prospect, some families like to comparison shop to see where they can get the best "deal." While this approach is an excellent way to find a new car or a needed appliance for the home, bargain priced puppies are no bargain. Standard expenses for breeding, whelping, and raising a litter do not change. Breeding a litter and raising it properly requires a significant investment of time, money, and love. Most reputable breeders do not make money on their litters. In fact, it is far more common that they lose money! Reputable breeders breed to help preserve the breed they cherish and to provide excellent examples of the breed for pet and show families to love. Because of this, their puppies will be priced higher than a puppy mill or backyard breeder's; however, you also have the assurance that the puppy came from parents who are both health tested and temperamentally sound. Reputable breeders will back their puppies with a health guarantee, and most will take back a puppy they have produced at any time and for any reason.

One of the biggest red flags you should look for is a breeder who will not permit you to come to their kennel to meet the parents of your future puppy or to see their facilities. Since puppy mill breeders often keep their adult dogs and puppies in unsanitary conditions, they want to keep you far away from their breeding operations.

Beware also of a breeder who does not know much about Shiba Inus. Reputable breeders love to talk about their breed and are happy to share their knowledge and training tips with you.

Among the conditions found at a puppy mill are:

- Cages that are overcrowded and too small for the dogs living in them.
- Cages that are stacked in a manner that proper air flow is not possible.
- Dogs living in unhygienic conditions, promoting serious illness and parasites.
- Repeated breeding of female dogs with no rest periods between litters.
- Continued breeding of aged dogs or dogs who are in ill health.
- Puppies separated from their mothers far too young.

Pet store Shiba Inus have most often come from puppy mill breeders.

What Should I Know About Shiba Inu Pet Store Puppies?

Though this practice is now banned in a lot of countries, there are still some pet stores which advertise and sell puppies. It has been reported by the Humane Society of the United States that up to 99% of all puppies for sale in pet stores are the product of puppy mills. Sadly, once these puppies fall into the hands of pet store owners, their prices are dramatically inflated, leading the unsuspecting buyer to think that they are purchasing a puppy from exceptional breeding practices. Unfortunately, this is quite far from the truth.

Reputable breeders of Shiba Inus will not allow a third-party agency to sell their puppies. It is important to them to get to know the families who will own one of their pups and to have the assurance that their puppy is going to an excellent home.

What Should I Know About Backyard Breeders?

Backyard breeders are different from puppy mills yet are still best avoided. Typically, a backyard breeder views breeding puppies as a hobby. While this in itself is not inherently wrong, most backyard breeders take no thought for health testing, correct conformation, or suitability of their dogs to be used as breeding stock. They know very little about their breed, and most often select breeding pairs based on whatever dogs are closest to their geographical location.

Not all purebred dogs are suited to be used in a breeding program. Only the very best dogs, who have passed rigorous health screening and who are of excellent temperament and conformation should be used to produce puppies.

A Final Word About Puppy Mills, Pet Store, and Backyard Breeders

The best way to eliminate puppy mills and backyard breeding is to refuse to support them. When the demand for low-priced puppies ceases, these unscrupulous breeders will no longer have any interest in continuing their operations since money is their primary goal.

When it comes to purchasing your Shiba Inu puppy, your heart may pull you a direction that is not wise for you to go. That is why you must always carefully do your research and temper the impulses of your heart with the wisdom you have accumulated in your head. You will be glad you waited to purchase your pup from a reputable Shiba Inu breeder.

CHAPTER 7

Getting Ready

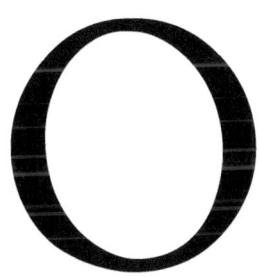

Once you have found the right Shiba Inu breeder for you, you should have an expected pick-up date for your puppy. Now is the time to start getting prepared for your new arrival! Having a few important items in place will help ease the transition for your new little bundle of joy.

A large part of getting ready for a puppy goes beyond picking up collars, leashes, food, and toys. You will need to begin by carefully evaluating your home to see which areas need to be changed to accommodate a mischievous baby puppy.

How Do I Puppy-Proof My Home for My Shiba Inu Puppy?

Most often, families will have a few weeks to a few months of preparation time prior to bringing their new puppy home. This time is invaluable to get your home ready for your new arrival. When evaluating your house, it is important to remember that a puppy's eyes rest at a different level than your own, meaning you might miss some things if you don't consider opportunities to wreak havoc that are right in your puppy's line of vision.

When beginning the puppy-proofing process, you will need to carefully assess each room of your house. Some common things which must be considered include:

- Trash cans in bathrooms and kitchens
- Compost bins
- Low lying cupboards containing cleaning agents and other chemicals
- Plants which are toxic to dogs
- Electrical cords and outlets
- Stairs

Puppies love to investigate new smells, and once they begin the teething process, they will also be on the hunt for things to sink their teeth into. This is why it is important to be certain that trash cans and compost bins are placed in areas where your puppy cannot access them. Alternatively, you can secure the lids with puppy-proof latches as a deterrent.

Trash cans and compost bins can contain materials that are toxic such as grapes and raisins, or that could pose a choking hazard such as large objects or bones. In addition to this, consumption of food waste is far too rich for a puppy's tummy and could lead to vomiting, diarrhea, or even pancreatitis.

Cupboards which can be accessed from your puppy's level can pose a particular temptation. Many cupboards contain cleaning materials with chemicals which are extremely caustic as well as toxic. If spilled on a mischievous puppy's skin, these chemicals could lead to nasty burns of the coat and skin. If ingested, they could end your puppy's life. To keep your Shiba puppy safe from cleaning agents and other items found in low-lying cupboards, you can purchase and install child-proof latches on the doors to keep them securely closed.

Though plants add a certain coziness and charm to a home, many of them are toxic to dogs and cats. Since puppies love to sink their chompers into things when they are teething, your household plants could easily become a target. If you have plants in your home that are toxic to dogs such as lilies, rhododendron, or poinsettias, it is wise to place them on shelves that your puppy cannot reach. Many families choose to "rehome" their plants as a safety precaution, rather than replace them with something that is pet-safe.

When getting your home ready for your puppy, always remember that your Shiba Inu puppy sees things from a different height perspective.

Electrical cords and outlets are particularly attractive to puppies. Since most of them sit on the ground or at eye level for a baby pup, your best course of action is to unplug anything that is not in use and to make use of plastic plugs to block access to open electrical currents.

If your home contains a lot of stairs, you will need to institute a plan to keep your baby Shiba from taking a tumble which could be very painful. Baby gates are an excellent means to keep your pup contained in a safe area. As your puppy begins to grow, navigating the stairs will become much easier. Before you know it, your pup will be racing down them like a pro!

How Do I Introduce My Shiba Inu Puppy to My Family and Other Pets? Shiba Inu and Cats–Do They Get Along?

Shiba Inu puppies love to be outdoors with their families.

If you have other pets in your home, you will want to exercise caution when introducing your new Shiba puppy to the rest of the family. Though it is human nature to want to lavish attention on the puppy, this could backfire, leading to resentment towards the puppy from other pet residents in the house.

It is important to note that many dogs and cats can feel territorial about their homes and their family. Fortunately, your Shiba puppy will receive patience and courtesy from your adult pets who recognize your pup's tender age and their role in shaping its future behavior. However, a well-thought out plan for introductions on your part will be much appreciated by your other pets and will go a long way to establishing a good relationship with the new puppy.

Introducing the puppy to its new family in a neutral location is often an excellent idea. It is also wise to allow your other pets to meet the puppy one at a time so as not to overwhelm your new Shiba puppy.

If you want to attempt early introductions at a neutral location, you can bring your puppy and your other pets to a public park where there are few other pets or distractions or even to your veterinarian's office. In some cases, your breeder will allow you to bring your other dogs to their home where they can assist you with introducing your puppy to its brothers and sisters in an isolated dog run or fenced area.

You can also introduce your puppy to its new siblings in the comfort of your fenced backyard. Regardless of which route you choose, it is important to proceed slowly, allowing the comfort of each pet involved to be your guide. The process may progress very smoothly with integration happening in one session, or it may take repeated attempts until everyone is comfortable with their new arrangement. There is no rush. Taking your time is to your advantage.

Even once your established pets have accepted their new sibling, it is important to carefully supervise all interactions between your adult pets and your new puppy. Puppies have a tendency to annoy older pets who may suffer with aches, pains, or other ailments which can cause them to snap at a silly puppy. Likewise, you must take care that your puppy isn't a persistent annoyance to the adult pets in its life.

What Shiba Inu Supplies Do I Need? Shiba Inu Gear

One of the most exciting parts of preparing for a new Shiba puppy is going shopping for all of the things that you will need. Though some items are best purchased with the puppy along to be properly fitted such as collars and clothing, there are many things that you can pick up in advance, so you are well-prepared for your puppy's arrival.

One of the first things you will need to purchase is bowls for your Shiba puppy's food and water. When it comes to food dishes, there is no specific brand or type that a Shiba Inu requires. Look for food and water dishes that are appropriate to your puppy's size, and that are made of materials that are pet-safe. Food and water dishes come in many different types of materials including ceramic, stainless steel, and plastic. Plastic is often not recommended since it can easily be chewed and swallowed by an overexuberant puppy.

Continuous feeding dishes are not recommended as free feeding can easily lead to serious weight gain in your Shiba puppy, causing excess strain on the joints of its rapidly growing body.

Avoid continuous feeding dishes to prevent your Shiba puppy from gaining too much weight.

No trip to the pet store for puppy supplies would be complete without the purchase of a collar or harness and a leash. However, since collars and harnesses require a very specific fit, it is a good idea to wait until your Shiba puppy comes home before making this type of purchase.

If you like, you can purchase your leash in advance of buying a collar. However, some families prefer to wait to buy both items at the same time, so they can color coordinate them.

Since Shiba Inu puppies love to chew, you will want to be sure you pick up a selection of toys for your pup to enjoy. Shiba Inus are small dogs, so you want to choose toys that are the right size for your pup. When purchasing toys, it is always a good idea to invest a little extra money to purchase items that are durable. Cheaper toys will break or shred more easily, and the small parts can easily be swallowed by your Shiba pup.

When selecting toys for your Shiba puppy, be certain to buy a wide variety of things in different shapes, sizes, textures, and colors. Your pup will soon display a preference for specific types of toys which will help you with purchases in the future.

Some families enjoy dressing their dogs up in sweaters, dresses, raincoats, and other novelty items. There is nothing wrong with doing this so long as your dog is a willing participant. Some dogs truly hate having to wear clothing, and if your puppy happens to fall into this category, it is best to leave the adorable doggy outfits at the store.

Other items which you will need to purchase for your new Shiba Inu puppy include:

- Puppy food
- Treats
- A crate

- Crate pads or other bedding
- Nail clippers or a Dremel
- A brush

Since nutrition, crate training, and grooming are important topics on their own, they will be discussed in greater detail in subsequent chapters.

Make sure to stock up on toys for your Shiba Inu, so your pup doesn't decide to create its own fun!

CHAPTER 8

Shiba Inu Nutrition

Selecting the right food for your Shiba puppy is very important. A high quality, nutritious diet will play an important role in the growth, development, and overall condition of your dog. Feeding the wrong kind of food can lead to health conditions such as obesity and can cause your otherwise healthy puppy to feel sluggish.

When you first bring your Shiba Inu puppy home, it is best to continue with whatever food your breeder was giving the pup. Your pup will face many new adjustments when transitioning from life at the breeder's home to yours. Introducing a new food to its system can cause great gastrointestinal distress and lead to diarrhea and vomiting.

Your breeder will send you home with a small amount of the puppy food they were feeding. Continue with that while you evaluate the food you feel is the best fit for your puppy. In this regard, your breeder can also be a help. Having bred, owned, and loved Shiba Inus for many years, the breeder will have important insights into what foods their own dogs have done well on.

If you opt to transition your puppy to a different brand of food, proceed cautiously. The best approach is to add some of the new food in with the old food at an approximate ratio of 2/3's of the old food to 1/3 of the new food. After a few days; assuming your puppy is tolerating this well, you can then change the measurements to ½ of the old to ½ of the new. Continue gradually increasing the amount of new food while decreasing the old food until the transition has been made. The entire process should take approximately one week to a week and a half.

What Are the Nutritional Requirements of Shiba Inus?

The Shiba Inu is considered a small breed dog, and thus, will do best when offered small meals more frequently throughout the day. As a general rule of thumb, aim to feed your puppy between three to four times daily. The amount will vary according to your puppy's activity level and the type of food being fed. The best course of action at this stage of life is to allow your puppy to eat as much as they want. In general, Shiba Inus are not prone to overeating, so excess weight gain is not a serious problem you will need to be concerned about.

As your puppy grows, its nutritional needs will change. You can adjust the amount and type of food you feed accordingly.

What is the Best Shiba Inu Food?

There is no specific food that is best suited to the Shiba Inu. However, it is vitally important that puppies eat puppy food. Puppy food is specifically formulated with the correct ratio of vitamins, minerals, nutrients, proteins, and carbohydrates to meet the demands of a puppy's developing body.

However, foods that are extremely high in protein can have a detrimental effect on your puppy's overall growth. It is best to select a puppy food that is no higher in protein than 29%. In addition to this, the type of protein included in your dog's food is also important. You want a diet that comes from the highest quality sources of meat, and that contains very little filler.

It is also wise to consider the amount of calcium included in any food you are considering feeding to your puppy. Too much calcium can promote rapid bone growth. While on the surface this would seem to be a good thing, bones that are growing too quickly can interfere with your puppy's structure as muscle development will still continue at the properly designated rate.

Your breeder and your veterinarian can best help you source the right puppy food for your Shiba. The most important components you are looking for is a product that is nutritionally balanced for your dog's age and size.

How Much Should I Feed My Shiba Inu?

Determining how much food your Shiba will need can be challenging. The amount of food you feed your puppy will be different from what an adult Shiba will require to maintain optimal health. But other factors influence the amount and frequency of food your Shiba will need.

One of the main considerations in determining how much food your dog requires is the quality of food you are feeding. Carefully read the ingredients list of your food to understand what is in it. The label on the packaging will also indicate a suggested amount for your dog's weight and size. This is an excellent guideline for you to follow.

Shiba Inus that are extremely active or underactive will need to have their food adjusted accordingly.

High quality nutrition is key to maintaining a healthy, happy Shiba.

What Should I Feed My Older Shiba Inu?

Senior Shiba Inus have different nutritional requirements than puppies or adults in the prime of their life. Since older dogs have a more difficult time processing protein, now is the time to transition your senior Shiba to a dog food formulation which has been designed to meet its specific needs.

Though you can continue to feed an adult dog food, it is recommended that you make the switch to something designed specifically for seniors. If your senior dog has experienced a decline in its activity level, you will also need to decrease the amount and the frequency of meals. Always feed your senior Shiba a minimum of two meals per day.

As with determining correct amounts for puppies or adults, the suggested serving sizes on the brand of food you purchase will offer you an excellent guideline. However, since your dog is a unique creature, you many need to adjust the amount of food you feed per meal until you find the right combination.

How Are Diet and Health Connected in Shiba Inus?

Diet and health are intricately linked when it comes to the well-being of your Shiba Inu. Feeding a poor-quality diet hinders energy levels and can lead to impairment of cognitive function and physical development.

Just as with children, the quality of the diet you feed will have a big impact on your Shiba Inu's overall health.

Is Dry Dog Food or Canned Dog Food Better for My Shiba Inu?

There are many different types of food available on the market today. Of the shelf-stable options, the two most popular varieties are dry food, also known as kibble, and wet food.

As a general rule, it is preferable to feed your Shiba Inu dry food. Wet food often contains far more calories than its dry counterpart, meaning it is far easier for your dog to overeat it. It is also much higher in fat than kibble.

In addition to this, kibble requires your dog to chew which results in some scrubbing action against the teeth which can help prevent the accumulation of plaque. Wet food sticks to the surface of the teeth which can promote dental decay and the formation of plaque.

Wet dog food is also considerably more expensive. It does have the added bonus of being particularly appetizing to most dogs. You can use it as a topper to stimulate your dog's appetite if your Shiba Inu is suddenly finding its regular kibble a little bland and boring.

What Should I Know About Raw Diets?

Raw diets are the latest trend in canine nutrition. Built upon the foundation that dogs in the wild were primarily carnivores, raw diets have their advantages and disadvantages.

Many veterinarians prefer that Shiba Inu puppy owners avoid this type of diet for several reasons. Raw diets require very rigorous handling and storage standards to prevent the development of food borne illness. But more important than this is where the meat is sourced from. If you opt to feed raw food, it is important that you buy a commercially prepared product or that you source the meat from a supplier who will sell you human grade proteins.

Many raw diets also encourage dogs to eat not just the meat but also the bone of the protein source. While raw chicken bones are not as likely to cause obstructions as their cooked counterparts, they do still splinter and can become lodged in the throat or even rupture your dog's intestines. This is an important factor to weigh when considering a switch to a raw diet.

However, there are also many benefits to this type of nutrition. The bones consumed by dogs in a raw diet are an excellent means of keeping your Shiba Inu's teeth clean. Oral health is vitally important to the longevity of your dog's life.

Raw food is also very appealing to many dogs who are otherwise quite picky.

The main thing to be aware of if you decide the raw diet is the right way to go for your Shiba Inu dog, is that the food you select is properly balanced with the correct formulation of vitamins and minerals to support optimal health.

Many Shiba Inus thrive on a raw diet.

What Do I Need to Know About Making Homemade Dog Food for My Shiba Inu?

Many dog owners consider making homemade dog food for their Shiba Inus. The advantage to homemade dog food is that you can carefully select the ingredients that go into it, giving you far more control. However, as with raw diets, homemade dog foods must have the proper balance of ingredients, vitamins, and minerals in order to be a healthy food choice for your dog.

If you opt to prepare your dog's diet yourself, take care to follow a recipe that has been formulated by a canine nutritionist. In addition to this, you will want to show your veterinarian the recipe you plan to use and carefully follow their advice to ensure the food your prepared has all of the necessary elements to support your dog's growth, health, and energy levels.

What are the Best Shiba Inu Dog Treats?

In general, Shiba Inus are not fussy dogs. However, some treats are better than others when it comes to maintaining your dog's health.

Biscuit type cookies are typically fairly low in calories, and they have a certain appeal when it comes to pooches. These treats are great to have on hand. Just be sure that the size you purchase is appropriate to the size of your dog to prevent overfeeding.

Meat-based treats such as jerkies or dehydrated proteins are extremely popular with dogs as well. These are higher value treats which are invaluable to use when training your Shiba. Limit the amount of these you dispense to prevent weight gain. It is best to reserve these treats for training sessions to maximize their appeal and increase your dog' interest in learning new things.

Small portions of pet-safe people foods can also be used as treats. Keep this practice to a minimum to prevent your dog from developing the habit of begging at the table.

What Foods are Dangerous to Shiba Inus?

There are no specific foods that are dangerous to Shiba Inus alone. However, there are several food items which are poisonous to all dog breeds. They are as follows:

- Grapes
- Raisins
- Onions
- Garlic

- Chocolate
- Xylitol
- Alcohol
- Avocados
- Macadamia nuts
- Yeast-based products

In addition to these items, bones can be dangerous as they can easily cause obstructions or become a choking hazard. Excess fatty items are also to be avoided as they can lead to pancreatitis, a painful condition which can be fatal.

CHAPTER 9

Shiba Inu Training

Though Shiba Inus can be challenging to train, that doesn't mean the process can't be fun! Shibas are incredibly intelligent. Since the breed is known for its independent thinking, you gain the opportunity to be creative to find interesting ways to help your dog see that learning can be a ball!

What Should I Know About Shiba Inu Training?

Shiba Inus are a breed that need to see training as something that will enrich their lives. Because they are in possession of a strong intellect coupled with a desire to be independent, it is not always easy to motivate a Shiba to willingly participate in training sessions.

To achieve the best results, it is wise to keep training sessions both short and lively. Since most Shibas love tasty treats, making use of a clicker and some delicious morsels of food provide an excellent incentive for your dog to want to work with you.

Shibas do not respond well to harsh training methods. However, they also will lose respect for an owner who is not consistent in what they expect or that is far too soft. A part of achieving this balance is teaching your dog that when you request an action, you expect to see it immediately. Repeating commands in an attempt to get the desired response will quickly teach your Shiba Inu that you are not serious, and they can blow you off and get away with it. This is best avoided by keeping your training sessions to only a few minutes and ending on a positive note. If your Shiba is feeling particularly stubborn, save training exercises for another day.

How To House Train Your Shiba Inu Puppy

Once you bring your Shiba Inu puppy home, the first thing you will need to do is housetrain it. There are many different ways to teach a puppy to do their business outdoors. The most effective method is through the use of a crate.

Since dogs naturally prefer to live in clean spaces, giving your Shiba puppy a crate that is all its own is an excellent means to teach your dog to keep its den free from bodily fluids and excrement.

The most effective way to house train your Shiba puppy using a crate is as follows:

- First thing in the morning, remove your puppy from its crate and carry the pup outside onto the grass. When your puppy eliminates or defecates in the correct spot, lavishly praise it.
- Once your puppy has done its business, you can bring your puppy indoors. Carefully supervise your pup; being cautious to take it outdoors again when you see signs of circling or after a rigorous playtime or nap. It is also important to take your dog out following meals. Reward your dog each time it does its business outdoors.

- When you cannot supervise your Shiba pup, place the pup inside its crate. Each time you allow the puppy out, immediately take the puppy outdoors and repeat the process of praising the pup for a job well done.

Over time, these steps will teach your dog the correct place to do their business. Of course, accidents will happen from time to time. When this occurs, it is important not to scold your puppy. Simply pick the puppy up and take them outdoors. Supervision and correct timing are key to helping your pup master housetraining.

Bear in mind that young puppies have not yet mastered control of their bladders. If left in their crates too long, your pup may have an accident in spite of trying its very best not to. This is where patience will be its own reward.

Some families prefer to forego using a crate in favor of using puppy pee pads. Most puppies are already familiar with them as many breeders make use of them when first familiarizing the puppies with housebreaking.

To house train a puppy using puppy pee pads, place the pee pad close to the door. Lavishly praise your puppy each time it goes to the pee pad and uses it. Over time, gradually move the pee pad to directly in front of the door, continuing to praise each time the puppy urinates or defecates in the correct spot. Eventually, you can move the pee pads outdoors then phase them out entirely when your puppy shows a pattern of reliably asking to be taken outdoors to its business.

Training Shiba Inu for Basic Obedience...Sit, Stay, and Come

There are three basic commands that all dogs should learn: sit, stay, and come. Though there are many other obedience cues that you could teach your dog, these three are critical as they have the potential to save your dog's life.

You will only need one tool to begin obedience training with your Shiba Inu: some super yummy treats. Reserve your dog's favorite snacks for training times to increase the likelihood that your dog will willingly work with you.

Teaching your dog to sit is the easiest of the three commands, as it is a natural default position for most dogs. To teach your dog to sit, hold the treat over your dog's head, so that it has to look up at you. For most dogs, this is sufficient for them to lower their rears to the ground naturally. If your dog does not do this, you can make use of your other hand to gently guide the dog into the sit position. As you do this, name the behavior "sit" and praise your dog for doing as requested. Repeat this command a few times, always rewarding with praise and treats when your dog complies. It will not take long before your dog begins to offer you a sit even before you request it!

The next command you should begin working on is stay. Stay is a very important command every dog should have in its trick repertoire. Since many dogs are killed each year when bolting from the open doors of their homes across busy streets, it is vital that your dog stay in position when asked to do so as it could save its life.

To teach a stay, ask your dog to assume the sit position, rewarding for the sit. Once in place, take one step away from your dog while repeating the word "stay." Step back in towards the dog and reward. When your dog displays that it is comfortable staying in position with you taking one step away, it is now time to attempt two steps away. Repeat this process, increasing distance until your dog shows the ability to stay in place when the command is issued. Stay is a particularly difficult command for a dog to learn, so you will want to celebrate when your dog willingly complies with what you ask it to do.

The final critical command is come. Just as you want your dog to stay in position to avoid danger; sometimes, it is necessary to ask your dog to come to you to get it out of harm's way. To teach the come command, ask your dog to sit then to stay. Walk across the room from your dog then turn to face it. In an excited voice, ask your dog to come, rewarding them with treats and praise when they obey.

When teaching the come command, it is very important that you never, ever scold a dog that comes to you. Though it is important to teach your dog that they must obey the first time they are asked not the tenth, the come command is the exception to this rule. If you get angry with a dog for not coming to you as soon as you ask it to, you will teach the dog that when it finally does come that it will be met with a negative reaction not a positive one. This, in turn, sets the dog up for failure in the future as dogs base their reactions on what their experiences have been for similar behaviors in the past. You want your dog to know that coming to you when called is the safest and best place to be.

Training your Shiba Inu can be a challenge, but with a little bit of creativity and some yummy treats, the process can also be lots of fun!

How to Train to Correct Bad Behavior

Shiba Inus are no different than any other breed when it comes to picking up bad habits. The best way to discourage bad behavior is to catch it early before it becomes ingrained in the dog's repertoire of things to do each day.

Since Shiba Inus respond very well to praise and treats, you can teach your dog to cease a behavior by refusing to reward it. This will require great consistency on your part. Some things our dogs get up to are extremely comical, and it is very hard to suppress a smile or a laugh. For this reason alone, you must learn to perfect the art of the poker face. Your dog is looking to you for a reaction. Even the stoic Shiba Inu wants to entertain you, and for this reason, you must give no sign that its bad behavior is comical to you.

Ignoring your dog's bad behavior will make the action seem quite dull to the dog over time. However, it is not enough to simply phase out bad behavior. You must then replace it with something you would prefer to see in its place. The best way to accomplish this is to reward alternate behaviors your dog offers that are pleasing to you. For example, if your dog likes to bark and jump up on you to get your attention, you must make a deliberate effort to refuse to engage with it in any way when the dog is acting in this fashion. When your dog ceases barking and approaches you calmly, you can then break out the treats and praise to teach your dog that the appropriate way to get your attention is through quiet, polite behavior. Over time, your dog will learn what works for it and what doesn't and will naturally begin to seek the actions that provide it with the best pay off.

Be sure to establish firm boundaries for your Shiba Inu to prevent bad habits from forming.

How Do I Train My Shiba Inu to do Tricks?

Training a Shiba Inu to do tricks follows the same protocols as obedience commands. With some delicious treats on hand and a willingness to learn, there is no limit to what your Shiba can do!

The internet has many different online viewing platforms where you can see videos instructions on training your dog to do different things. There are also several books available online and in stores.

Avoiding Aggression

Though the Shiba Inu can be prone to dog aggression, there are steps that you can take to avoid this from becoming a problem for your dog. The most important thing you can do to help your dog see other dogs as friends and not foes is to begin socializing it with other socially appropriate dogs as young as possible. However, the importance of only allowing social opportunities between dogs with exceptional manners cannot be overstated. Your Shiba puppy will continue to learn from the dogs it is allowed to spend time with. Set your puppy up for success by only allowing it to spend time with dogs that have a proven track record of playing well with other dogs.

It is important to note that dog aggression can occur in the breed, and thus, it may not be possible to prevent it in your dog. However, choosing a puppy from a breeder whose lines are known for dog friendliness as well as early socialization can help prevent dog aggression from becoming something you have to deal with on an ongoing basis.

Socialization—Why It is Important and How to Do It

Proper socialization is key to a well-adjusted dog. Socialization is essentially the process of introducing your dog to the things that will be a part of its life on a daily basis.

This process should be started in the breeder's home as early as three days of age when the puppies are primed to experience early neurological stimulation. This set of protocols relies on the introduction of novel experiences through the sense of touch to help a puppy become accustomed to responding appropriately to new things.

Since baby puppies are sponges that are ripe for learning, it cannot be emphasized how important it is to introduce them to as many new experiences as possible during their first 16 weeks of life. However, care must be taken that these new situations are positive only. Young puppies are very much undergoing a formative period during which all experiences can leave a lasting imprint. One negative interaction at this time is often all it takes for a puppy to view that particular thing with fear or even aggression for the remainder of its life.

Most breeders recommend that you continue the socialization process through attending an organized puppy socialization class. This is an excellent means to encourage appropriate to dog to dog interactions as well as to begin learning canine skills. However, socialization does not stop here. To help facilitate the learning process, take your puppy to as many safe places as you can including the pet store, your vet's office, through the drive thru, on car rides, on walks, etc. This will help your puppy to continue learning that new things are exciting and fun instead of something to be feared.

Should your puppy have a bad experience on a social outing, do not make a big deal out of it. If you coddle the pup or force it to remain in the situation, you will deepen the fear which is counterproductive. After a scare, simply remain cheerful and happy, removing your pup to a new and more positive environment.

Biting—Why Dogs Do It and How to Avoid It

Biting is a common problem that should be addressed when your Shiba is yet a puppy. There are several reasons why dogs may bite. The first reason is because that is the way that dogs first learn to explore their world. Their first interactions are with their littermates, and it is during these times that they learn bite inhibition.

Bite inhibition is essentially the process that teaches a puppy to use its mouth appropriately. Puppies mouth when they play, and if they bite a litter mate too strongly, they will be rebuked for it, thus teaching them to use less force next time or suffer the consequences.

The second reason puppies bite is to alleviate pain they are experiencing in their mouths. Teething is most often the cause of this. During this phase, you will often see a puppy attempting to sink its teeth into anything that appears to be plush or that has some give. This can include your hand!

The best way to teach your dog not to bite is to react strongly whenever its teeth come into contact with your skin. If you yell,

"OUCH!" when you are bitten, your puppy will be alarmed and will soon come to understand that this behavior is not acceptable.

Another method to curb biting is redirection. When your puppy attempts to bite you or an object you would prefer it not, you can simply direct the dog to something more appropriate for chewing like a dog toy or a bone.

As with most behaviors, biting is best addressed in the puppy years. Preventing a problem is far better than having to try to rehabilitate an adult dog, a task which can often prove to be impossible.

Positive Reinforcement Training

Positive reinforcement training is essentially the use of treats and praise as rewards to motivate a dog to learn. Since Shibas need an incentive to work and assimilate new skills, positive reinforcement training is the ideal method to use in your training sessions with your new puppy.

Teaching your dog new skills using positive reinforcement techniques requires good timing. If you wish to teach your dog to sit, you can use a treat as a lure to get your dog into the correct position. While your dog is moving into a sitting position, you then name the action "Sit" then reward when the dog complies with your command. It is easy to see that the timing of naming the action then rewarding it is key to your dog's learning.

Clicker Training

Clicker training is essentially the same as positive reinforcement training except instead of using verbal praise to reinforce a behavior, you teach your dog that the sound of the clicker means a job well done. As with positive reinforcement techniques, clicker training relies primarily on praise and delicious treats to reward the dog for offering the correct behavior when asked to do so.

CHAPTER 10
Shiba Inu Health

Keeping your Shiba Inu healthy is one of your top priorities as an owner. The first course of action that promotes the achievement of the ideal health and wellness of your dog is finding a veterinarian that you can trust.

How Do I Find a Veterinarian for My Shiba Inu Puppy?

If you don't already have a veterinarian, you can begin your search by asking your friends who own dogs which clinic they frequent and why. Peer recommendations can go a long way to helping you narrow down the list of potential veterinary clinics to care for your Shiba's health.

With so many online platforms now offering reviews, you can also search the internet for opinions about any clinic or doctor you may be considering. When doing this, it is important to remember that reviews are one-sided and often not fair. However, if there are 100 reviews and 90 of them are unfavorable, it is safe to assume that that clinic is likely one to avoid.

Your breeder may also have a recommendation for you. Even if your breeder does not live in your area, chances are quite good that he or she has placed puppies with other families who live near to you. These families' experiences with their vets in neighboring clinics can help you narrow down the playing field in your search for the right clinic for your dog.

What Should I Know About Vaccines for My Shiba Puppy?

Following a thorough vaccination schedule for your Shiba puppy is a critical component of protecting it against disease. If your puppy leaves your breeder's home at eight weeks of age, it should already have received its first set of core vaccinations. Along with your puppy, you should have received a health certificate and a booklet which details all vaccinations, flea preventatives, and de-wormings as well as dates for when the next set of shots is due.

Here is a general guideline which outlines a thorough vaccination schedule for a Shiba puppy:

Puppy Age	Recommended Vaccines	Optional Vaccines
7-8 weeks	Distemper, parvovirus, parainfluenza	Bordetella
10-12 weeks	DHPP (vaccines for distemper, adenovirus [hepatitis], parainfluenza, and parvovirus)	Coronavirus, Leptospirosis, Bordetella, Lyme disease
12-24 weeks	Rabies (not required in the UK)	None
14-16 weeks	DHPP	Coronavirus, Lyme disease, Leptospirosis

Puppy Age	Recommended Vaccines	Optional Vaccines
12-16 months	Rabies (not required in the UK), DHPP	Coronavirus, Lyme disease, Leptospirosis
Every 1-2 years	DHPP	Coronavirus, Lyme disease, Leptospirosis
Every 1-3 years	Rabies (not required in the UK)	None

Will My Shiba Inu Puppy Have His First Vaccines While at the Breeder's Home?

Every reputable breeder will want their puppies to be protected against the core diseases that could negatively impact a puppy's health while its immunity is still in progress. For this reason, no puppy should leave the breeder's home without having had its first shot in the series of core vaccines.

It is important to follow the vaccination schedule established by your breeder and your veterinarian.

What Are Common Diseases Affecting the Shiba Dog Breed?

In general, the Shiba Inu is a relatively healthy breed with few genetic health ailments that are of concern. However, it is important for you to know ahead of time some of the illnesses and conditions which can prove problematic in the breed.

The most commonly seen problems in Shiba Inus are:

- Hip dysplasia
- Elbow dysplasia
- Glaucoma
- Von Willebrand's disease
- Patellar luxation (dislocation of the kneecap)
- Neuronal Ceroid Lipofuscinosis
- Uveodermatologic (VKH syndrome)

Hip and Elbow Dysplasia in Shiba Inus

Both hip and elbow dysplasia are inherited genetic conditions which can affect the Shiba Inu. Dysplasia occurs when the dog's joints are not properly formed. The disease is incredibly painful and can lead to premature arthritis and crippling. The disease is first evidenced when the dog begins to show sign of lameness, pain, or an unwillingness to place any weight upon the affected limb.

Treatment for hip or elbow dysplasia is pain medication or surgery if quality of life is deeply impacted. Arthritis will occur in dogs suffering from hip or elbow dysplasia with the signs becoming more evident, even in young dogs, with growth and development.

Dogs suffering from hip or elbow dysplasia must be kept at a healthy weight to avoid aggravating the condition.

Both hip and elbow dysplasia can be tested for, and animals who do not receive a rating of "Good" or higher should be eliminated from any breeding program for the health of future generations.

Common Eye Problems and the Shiba Inu

There are two main eye diseases for which Shiba Inu are at risk: glaucoma and Uveodermatologic syndrome (VKH syndrome). Testing can be done via a canine opthalmologist to determine the health of the eyes of the puppies and their parents. Any dog that does not receive a passing grade on their eye test should not be used for breeding.

Glaucoma is an eye disorder which affects canines and humans. The disease is very painful and can cause blindness if not treated properly. Early diagnosis is critical to helping preserve proper functionality of the eye. However, the initial stages of glaucoma are very difficult to diagnose and replicate other seemingly harmless problems such as dust in the eye or allergies.

The main symptoms of glaucoma include watery eyes, squinting, redness of the white of the eye, and swollen or bulging eyes. Opthalmologists consider glaucoma a medical emergency, so at the first signs of a problem, it is vital that you get your Shiba to the vet for diagnosis and treatment.

Uveodermatologic syndrome, also known as VKH syndrome, is seen more frequently in Shiba Inus than in other breeds. This disease is a type of autoimmune disorder which affects the eyelids and skin surrounding the eye. VKH syndrome is extremely painful and can cause blindness. Over time, pigment is lost in sensitive areas of the face including the nose, eyes, and lips. Exposure to the sun exacerbates the condition.

Von Willebrand's Disease in Shiba Inus

Von Willebrand's disease is a genetically inherited bleeding disorder. There are degrees of severity of this condition which can range from mild to life threatening.

This disease often goes undetected until the dog sustains an injury, and it is discovered that its blood will not clot. DNA testing is available to detect carriers of the disease. Any dog which tests as a carrier should not be bred to another dog who also carries the gene mutation. Affected dogs should never be bred.

Patellar Luxation in the Shiba Dog

Patellar luxation is essentially the slipping of the kneecap out of its socket. It is extremely painful when it occurs and can lead to further complications such as meniscal tears or torn cruciates, two medical problems which require expensive surgeries to repair with long wait times for proper recovery.

Luxating patellas are often evidenced when the dog begins to run then hops for several strides before resuming a regular pace. Luxating patellas are graded in degrees. At their lowest levels, they may be mildly uncomfortable and an inconvenience at best. However, anything higher than that can lead to extreme discomfort and tremendous pain. Surgery is possible; however, it is not recommended.

The patellas of any dog being considered for a breeding program should be subject to testing by a veterinarian. If the patella will luxate at all under manipulation, the dog should no longer be eligible for breeding.

Neuronal Ceroid Lipofuscinosis in the Shiba Inu

Neuronal Ceroid Lipofuscinosis, also referred to as NCL, is a disease which affects the nerves. It is most typically seen in young dogs of approximately one to three years or age.

The most common signs include weakness of the rear legs and difficulty balancing. Some dogs also experience blindness.

There is no treatment for NCL; however, genetic testing is available to determine if a dog is a carrier or affected.

Allergies in the Shiba Inu

As with many other dog breeds, the Shiba Inu can be prone to developing allergies. Keeping a clean coat is one of the most important ways you can help to prevent skin conditions and allergies from occurring. However, some Shibas will experience allergic reactions to their environment or specific food sensitivities. Though veterinarians can do some sensitivity testing, it is typically limited to food allergens. Even so, identifying food triggers which are causing your dog to experience allergy flareups can be helpful in pinpointing foods you should avoid.

If your Shiba's allergies are persistent and are affecting its quality of life, there are several medications your dog can take to alleviate its symptoms. Each must be prescribed by a veterinarian, with routine bloodwork conducted several times throughout the year measure the drug's efficacy as well as its effects on your dog's liver and kidneys.

CHAPTER 11

Shiba Grooming

P art of keeping your Shiba Inu looking top notch includes regular grooming. Though the Shiba has fewer grooming requirements than other coated breeds, it still does require some effort to keep your dog's coat in excellent condition. The quality of your dog's coat will be greatly impacted by the quality of nutrition it is fed regularly. But it is not just nutrition that shapes the character of the Shiba coat. The thickness and integrity of your dog's fur comes down to a combination of genetics, diet, and regular coat care.

Thankfully, the Shiba Inu is not a high maintenance dog when it comes to grooming. In fact, with only a very few tools in place, you can manage all of your dog's coat care all on your very own!

Regular grooming will help keep your Shiba's coat in tip top shape.

Shiba Inu Grooming Tools

The Shiba Inu has been affectionately referred to as a "wash and wear" dog because of its low maintenance grooming requirements. However, to keep your dog's coat and skin both healthy and clean, it is important to give your dog regular baths.

You will not require any special tools to groom your Shiba Inu. All you need is a good quality pet shampoo, a blow dryer, and a brush.

What Do I Need to Know About Shiba Inu Bathing? Is There a Specific Shiba Inu Shampoo?

There is no particular shampoo that is best for the Shiba Inu coat. If you notice your Shiba's skin is particularly sensitive or dehydrated, it is best to use something gentle with moisturizing properties such as a shampoo that is enriched with oats and aloe.

Most breeders recommend that the Shiba be bathed only twice yearly. If your Shiba rolls in mud or something more sinister, it will be necessary to bath more frequently than that. However, as a general rule, bathing too often can dehydrate the skin, leading to itchiness and skin discomfort. Always be certain to thoroughly rinse out any soap debris from your Shiba's coat as failure to do this can lead to itchiness as well.

It is not necessary to blow dry your Shiba Inu. Air drying is typically sufficient. However, if you prefer to dry your Shiba yourself, simply use a blow dryer on a moderate setting, taking care to brush the hair in the direction of the hair growth.

What Do I Need to Know About Shiba Inu Toenail Care?

Shiba Inus typically do not like people handling their feet, making toenail care a bit of a challenge. If you frequently walk your dog on hard surfaces, you will discover that the dog has naturally done most of the work for you. However, maintaining toenails that are the correct length are an important part of keeping your dog healthy and well.

To help set your dog up for success, it is best to introduce them to the nail care process when still a baby puppy. Your breeder will have begun this job for you by regularly trimming nails with clippers as young as only a few days old. Over time, many breeders switch to a handheld sanding device as this allows them to take the nails shorter and reduces the risk of pain or injury from nicking the quick of the dog's nails.

Shibas can be divas about nail trims, an activity that will sometimes elicit the distinctive sound referred to as the "Shiba scream." If this should occur, remain calm and continue to work quietly and steadily.

Should you happen to nick the quick of your dog's nails, you will find that Shibas have long memories and are quick to throw a dramatic fit the next time you attempt a nail trimming. If this is the pattern you see with your dog, it may be best to take your Shiba to a groomer or to the vet when it is time for its nails to be done.

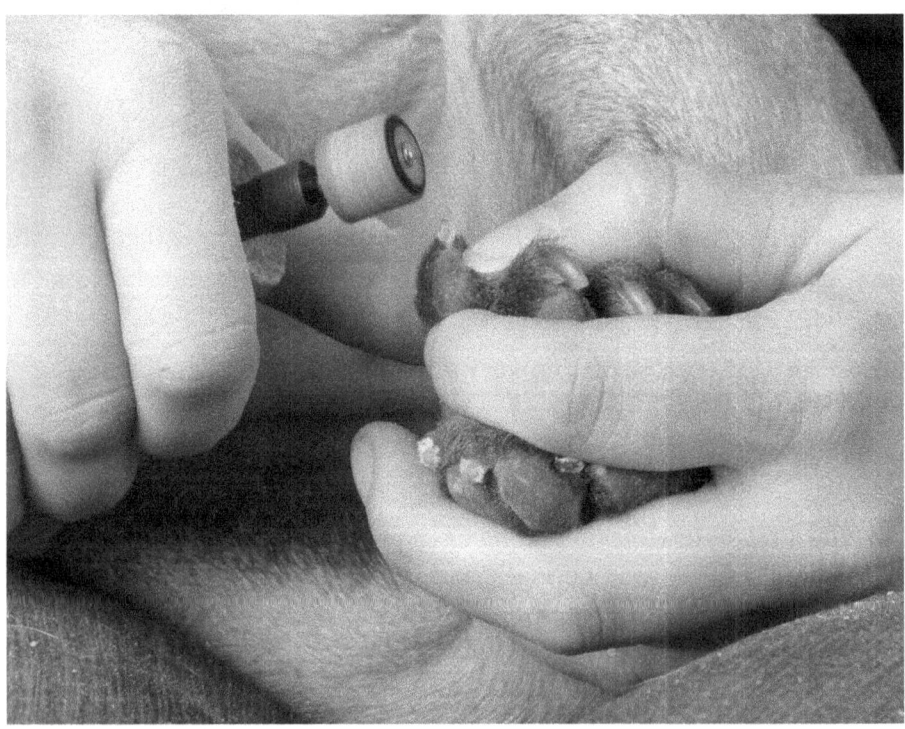

Nail care is an important part of grooming the Shiba Inu.

What Do I Need to Know About Shiba Inu Dental Care?

Keeping up with regular teeth cleaning is an important part of helping your Shiba Inu to remain healthy. The best means to prevent the accumulation of plaque is by regular tooth brushing with a pet safe toothpaste. This can be obtained from your veterinarian's office.

But proper dental care involves more than just the teeth, attention should also be paid to the health of the gums of your Shiba. Some owners like to purchase a tooth scaler to help them gently move plaque from under the gum line and off the teeth. However, this can leave tiny chips in the enamel. If plaque accumulation under the gumline has occurred, it is best to take your Shiba Inu dog to your veterinarian for a teeth cleaning.

Other preventative means to keep your Shiba's teeth pearly white include raw meaty bones and water additives.

What Do I Need to Know About Shiba Inu Ear Care?

Since the Shiba Inu has small prick ears, the breed is not prone to ear infections. Cleaning is rarely required to maintain optimal health of the ear. However, if you notice a distinct odor coming from that region, it is best to take your dog to the vet to rule out any possible infection.

Cleaning your dog's ears is not a difficult task; however to most effectively get the job done, it is best for you to have an in-person demonstration by your veterinarian.

CHAPTER 12

Showing a Shiba

Showing your Shiba Inu can be lots of fun. One of the benefits of entering your Shiba in shows is the opportunity to see more examples of the breed to see how your dog measures up against the best of the best in your area. But more than this, you will gain the opportunity to make new friends in the breed who can assist you in your quest to learn more about your beloved Shiba.

Showing your Shiba Inu can be a lot of fun.

What Do I Need to Know About the AKC Shiba Inu?

There are seven groups that each recognized dog breed is categorized into in the American Kennel Club. Each of the breeds within a group should bear some similarities in purpose, origins, or appearance. The Shiba Inu falls within the Non-Sporting Group, pitting him against breeds such as the Standard Poodle, the French Bulldog, the Dalmatian, and the Bichon Frise.

When looking at the list of non-sporting breeds, you might ask yourself how in the world a judge could compare a Shiba Inu to a Poodle to declare a winner. That is an excellent question.

When judges judge any particular breed, they judge the dog against its own standard. This means that the judge that examines your Shiba will look at the established standard of what traits the ideal Shiba should have and how your dog measures up against it. This judge will do this in turn with all of the dogs entered in your breed class. The winner is the dog who most closely resembles the standard, and that dog is awarded a ribbon and the title of Best of Breed.

If your dog has been selected Best of Breed, it will then go on to compete with all of the other Best of Breed winners in the Non-Sporting group where the top 4 dogs will receive group placements. At this time, the judge is still comparing your Shiba against its own standard. He is also considering the Poodle against the Poodle standard and the Bichon against the Bichon standard, and so on and so forth. The dogs in the group who are the best examples of their own breed when compared against the other breed representatives are awarded accordingly. So if the

Dalmatian is the dog in the ring that most closely matches its own standard, the Dalmatian is awarded the Gr 1st. If the Bichon is the second closest, that dog become the 2nd place winner and so and so forth. The winner of the Non-Sporting group then proceeds on to Best in Show to compete against the top winners in each of the seven groups.

There are several breed characteristics which are considered a disqualification in Shiba Inus. They are as follows:

- Males who are over 16.5"(42 cm) or under 14.5" (37 cm).
- Females who are over 15.5" (39 cm) or under 13.5" (34 cm).
- A bite that overshot or undershot (overbite or underbite).

Any dogs exhibiting these traits would be asked to leave the ring.

Can Any Shiba Inu Be Shown at a Dog Show?

Not all dogs are eligible to be shown at an AKC show. If you wish to show your dog, you must first purchase a dog that is registered. While it is simplest to obtain a dog that already has its AKC registration, you can purchase a puppy from a foreign breeder who registers their dogs with a different kennel club. You can then begin the process of securing an AKC registration; however, the process is lengthier, more expensive, and more difficult.

The one kennel club whose registration is not accepted by the AKC is the Continental Kennel Club.

Though any registered purebred Shiba Inu can be shown in dog shows, not all of them should be. Within every litter, there will be some excellent examples of the breed, and some, who for one reason or another, are considered pet quality. This does not in any way mean that the dog is inferior; it simply means it is suited to a different purpose.

Showing is an exceptionally expensive hobby, and those who do enter dog shows hope to bring home ribbons at the end of the day. Entering a Shiba who differs from the breed standard in any significant way is bound to lead to disappointment. But even if your Shiba isn't quite right for the show ring, there are still lots of fun things you can do with your dog. You can even participate and earn titles in such AKC registered events as Rally, Obedience, and Agility.

How Do I Select a Good Shiba Inu Puppy to Compete in Dog Shows?

Selecting a Shiba Inu puppy to compete in dog shows involves wise decisions amongst knowledgeable experts in the breed. Your best resource to accomplish this goal is your breeder. Most reputable breeders do breed dogs with the intent of showing them, and thus, reserve the puppies who most closely reflect their standard to go to show homes.

If this is something that you think you might like to do, be sure to tell your breeder ahead of time that you are interested in a show quality puppy. Be aware that show quality puppies often cost substantially more than pet quality puppies, and you may need to wait a longer period of time to obtain one.

What Coat Colors are Accepted in the AKC Shiba?

The coat colors accepted by the AKC include: red, red sesame, cream, and black and tan.

Are Shiba Inus Good for Dog Sports Competitions and Agility Contests?

Though Shiba Inus can be a handful to train, they are well-suited to dog performance sports such as Agility, Rally, and Obedience.

CHAPTER 13

Working Shiba Inus

Shiba Inus were originally intended to function as working dogs, assisting their owners on such important activities at hunting and providing oversight of the home and hearth. Today, the Shiba Inu has largely made the move towards being a beloved house pet. Still this is one dog breed that remains true to its working roots and that thrives when given a job to do.

The Shiba Inu excels at many different jobs.

The Shiba Inu Therapy Dog

Though Shiba Inu can be aloof with strangers, its friendly nature and calm ways make it an ideal candidate for therapy dog work. A dog not prone to overexuberance, Shiba Inus can be taught to be polite and well-mannered, making them well-suited to nursing home visits to brighten the days of the elderly.

The Shiba Inu Police Dog

Shiba Inu are in possession of excellent scent detection capabilities, making them a good choice for police or military work which involves the unearthing of drugs through the use of scent alone. The Shiba Inu is also a courageous dog, giving it a willingness to follow its fellow colleagues into areas where danger is suspected.

Shiba Inus were originally working dogs who still enjoy having a job to do.

Shiba Inu Guard Dog

One of the original purposes of the Shiba Inu was to provide guardianship over the home and estate of its family The Shiba is bold and full of confidence. Though this breed will not initiate aggressive behavior, the Shiba will respond to anything it perceives as a threat against its family or its home.

CHAPTER 14

Breeding

The decision to breed your Shiba Inu should not be undertaken lightly. You are making a commitment for the life of any litters you produce, so you want to be certain you have done your homework and are fully prepared for the responsibilities that come with breeding Shiba Inus.

The first step you should take in preparing to breed is learning all that you can about the Shiba Inu. Your puppy buyers will come to you looking for wisdom and advice about from everything from grooming to nutrition to training and more. You want to be certain you have the necessary experience to properly guide them as they raise your puppy.

Secondly, not all purebred, registered Shiba Inus are suitable for breeding. The chapter on health can help you understand what health tests must be performed and passed on your breeding dog to qualify him or her for a breeding program. Though most Shiba Inu national breed clubs recommend only testing for hip and elbow dysplasia and potential eye diseases, a wise breeder will seek out opportunities to conduct the most thorough health testing options available and make their breeding decisions according to the results. Should your Shiba fail even one of the required health tests or receive a substandard score, it is best to eliminate that particular dog from your breeding plans for the future health of the breed.

But it is not only health that factors into what makes a dog eligible for breeding though it is of paramount importance. You must ask yourself what it is about your dog that has you considering breeding him or her. Does your dog have an exceptional temperament? That is a must in a breeding dog. How well does your dog match up to your standard? Does he or she have any serious faults? Does your dog have any attributes that are considered a disqualification for a judge? All of these factors should be very carefully weighed prior to breeding. If your dog does not have any qualities that are outstanding and that can contribute to the betterment of the breed, your dog may be better suited to life as a beloved family pet than a breeding dog.

Shiba Inu breeding is a serious responsibility which should not be undertaken lightly.

How Do I Find a Mate for My Shiba Inu?

Finding the right mate for your Shiba Inu can prove a challenge. The most important step you must make is a careful analysis of your dog to see what areas you would like to improve on in your dog's puppies. No dog is perfect, so it is not an insult to your Shiba to make a list of two or three areas for improvement.

Once you have done this, the next thing to do is to start looking around to see what other Shibas are out there that would complement your dog. This can be a difficult process and can take many months or even years. There is no rush, so take your time to make your choice. Carefully consider each dog that is available and do your due diligence to ensure that all appropriate health testing has been completed and passed in any dog that you are considering using in your breeding program.

It is always a good idea to ask another experienced Shiba breeder for advice once you have narrowed down your selection to a few dogs. In this way, you gain access to a second set of eyes that can confirm your decision or help you see things you have overlooked that could make the pairing less than what you had hoped for.

When you have made your final decision, it is time to approach the owner of the other dog for permission to use their dog in your breeding program. Take the time to properly introduce yourself and to share photos, any important wins, and the health testing on your own dog.

Be prepared to pay a stud fee for the service provided. This is not a negotiable amount of money. The owner sets the price, and you pay what is asked. Some owners will want the money up front while others are willing to wait until after the stud service has been rendered or puppies are on the ground. These are all details that can be decided upon mutually then written up in a contract for you both to agree to and sign.

In some cases, an owner would prefer to take the pick puppy of the litter in lieu of a stud fee. Some breeders prefer to avoid this, particularly if they breed for the show ring. It is entirely up to you and the owner of the stud dog as to what you feel is best.

What is the Shiba Inu Heat Cycle?

Heat cycles vary from dog to dog, but typically, Shibas will cycle twice per year for a period that can last up to 30 days. Most often, a Shiba will experience her first heat cycle between six to eight months of age. However, she will not be mature enough physically or emotionally to whelp and raise a litter of her own until after her second birthday.

There are several signs which can indicate your Shiba's season is soon approaching. One of the most common signs is swelling of the vulva which is accompanied by a bloody vaginal discharge. This will soon turn to a straw color when your dog begins her approach on the days when she is most fertile and ready to be bred.

Though a dog's heat cycle usually lasts 30 days, she is not fertile this entire time. Progesterone testing can be conducted at your vet to help you pinpoint the best days to attempt a breeding. This is particularly important if you have to do any travelling to reach the stud dog or if you are using fresh or frozen semen at a veterinary clinic for an artificial insemination. Your female's peak fertility season most often lasts between 4-7 days at a maximum.

What Should I Know About the Shiba Inu Mating Process?

Most often, your Shiba Inu female will let you know when she is ready to be bred. The urge to reproduce is exceptionally powerful in dogs, and when the time is upon your girl, she will begin to flirt with any male dog that comes her way. The dog that previously snapped at your male who just sniffed her rear in passing will now shove her private parts directly in his face with her tail flagging to the side as a not so subtle hint.

When it comes time to bring the male and female dog together, you should stay with the dogs in case your assistance is needed. If you bring the dogs together too early in the heat cycle, the male dog may not be interested, and you will need to try again another day. Male dogs possess an extremely sensitive sense of smell, and an experienced stud dog can tell when a female is ready to be bred. Trust him and his instincts.

If your dog is a maiden, she may become scared when the male dog attempts to mount her. Your presence will be comforting to her, particularly if the two dogs tie, and you need to keep both dogs calm while you wait for the tie to end.

What Should I Know About Shiba Inu Pregnancy?

All pregnancies, regardless of breed, are 63 days from the point of conception. But since most breeders breed over a period of several days, it can be difficult to pinpoint exactly which days the puppies will arrive. The best course of action is to count 63 days from each tie and mark them on your calendar as the potential dates for your girl's litter of puppies.

During your dog's pregnancy, life will proceed as normal. Your dog will begin to grow a belly, and her nipples will become engorged with the milk that she will feed her puppies once they are born.

It is best to limit activity to things within your home to avoid your pregnant dog from coming in contact with anything that could be harmful to her and her puppies.

How Do I Help to Prepare My Shiba Inu to Give Birth?

There are some preparations you must be make in anticipation of the arrival of your dog's puppies. A week or so in advance of the first possible due date, you should set up the area where your dog will give birth. It should be a spot that is quiet, private, and dark to help your dog feel safe and secure while she whelps her babies.

You will need a whelping box that is the right size for your dog and her offspring. The box should be large enough to give her room to get up and move around while still small enough that her puppies will not get lost if they move away from their mother.

You will want to line the whelping box with puppy pads, old sheets, or paper that can be thrown away. The birthing process is messy and can stain bedding, so take care to use things that you don't mind throwing away after the whelping process is done. Be sure the materials you include are clean and comfortable for your mother dog and her puppies.

It is important to be sure your female dog is healthy and mentally sound enough to whelp and raise a litter.

What Should I Know About Shiba Inu Labor and Delivery?

The first step in the birthing process is identifying the signs that labor is imminent. When your dog begins to nest in the box you have prepared for her, you will know that it is nearly time for puppies to be born.

Other signs you may see are:

- Heavy panting
- Pacing
- Anxiety

Your dog may also try to find a dark place outsider her pen where she can hide to birth her young. For this reason; if your dog needs a bathroom break, take her out on a leash to avoid her hiding in a hard to reach place.

Dogs instinctively know what to do when it comes to the whelping process. However, it is good for you to be close by in case your girl runs into any trouble.

How Do I Care for Newborn Shiba Inu Puppies?

When the puppies are newly born, there is very little work for you to do. The mother dog will care for all of their needs. During the first two weeks of life, your Shiba puppies will be both blind and deaf. They will depend entirely on their mother for all of their needs, a role she will fulfill perfectly.

Around three weeks of age, the puppies' eyes and ears will be fully open, and they will begin to try to toddle around. It is during this period that they gain the ability to urinate and defecate on their own, and your work as a breeder will begin.

Most reputable breeders have an established waiting list for their puppies, so homes are lined up well in advance of the puppies' arrival. If you have a few puppies that do not yet have homes, now is the time to begin your search for the right families for them. Your Shiba breeder can be an invaluable help to you in this process, providing you with contacts and avenues to explore.

Shiba Inu puppies require little work from the breeder during their first two weeks of life.

CHAPTER 15

Shiba Inu Mixes

Shiba Inus have so many wonderful qualities that many people want to breed them to other dog breeds in the hopes they will pass along some of their most endearing traits. Today, hybrids or designer dogs are increasing in popularity, driving a trend of more mixes of two different breeds to achieve a dog capable of fulfilling a desired purpose. Though some people simply choose to combine two different purebred breeds together with the sole purpose of creating a wonder dog that will make them lots of money, most breeders of designer dogs put a lot of thought and care into the dogs they select for breeding. They carefully do their research to match together two purebred breeds who have the potential to make an excellent pairing. They back this with appropriate health testing for both dog breeds to promote optimal health in the resulting puppies.

Though cross-breeding of Shiba Inus is a relatively new phenomenon, there are several hybrids which have gained popularity.

Husky Inu

The offspring of a Siberian Husky and a Shiba Inu are most commonly referred to as Husky Inus. By breeding these two purebred dog breeds together, you gain a dog that is visually stunning and that closely resembles a wolf, the ancient ancestor of the Shiba Inu.

The combining of these two breeds can result in a dog that is fiercely independent and in possession of immense prey drive. Since both Huskies and Shiba Inus are prone to easy escapes, a secure fence is a must for this hybrid.

The Husky Inu definitely requires an experienced owner as they can be quite difficult to train. In general, the breed is quite reserved with people and prefers to keep to itself, making it a poor selection for families seeking a dog for companionship.

Shih Poms

The offspring of a Shiba Inu mixed with a Pomeranian are referred to as Shi Poms or Pom Shis. These two dogs are dramatically different in both personality and size, making for an interesting blend of these two breeds. The ideal traits breeders of the Shiba Inu Pomeranian hope to achieve is a dog that is a quieter Pomeranian or a more outgoing Shiba.

Because this hybrid is very new in its development, many inconsistencies remain in the offspring. The ideal Shi Pom is intended to be a dog that is friendly and loyal; however, many of them remain true to their Pomeranian roots and can be spirited and prone to barking.

In physical appearance, the Shi Pom remains small in size, weighing in between 12-14 pounds (5-6 kg). In height, the dog is 9"-12" (23-30 cm) at the withers. Coat colors range from tan to tan and white, black and white, and black and tan.

Shiba Retriever

The Shiba Retriever, also sometimes referred to as the Golden Shiba, is a mixed breed comprised of a Shiba Inu and a Golden Retriever. Both dog breeds hail from hunting origins, a trait which is well-established in this cross breed. Because of their immense prey drive, the potential is great for this hybrid to view smaller animals as hunting targets. To prevent this from becoming a problem, a Shiba Retriever puppy should be introduced to other family pets at a young age to help them view the other pet residents as siblings and not prey.

As a newly developed cross breed, the Shiba Retriever does not yet have a consistently defined personality. Some puppies gravitate more towards the gentle, loving personality of the Golden while other are more reserved, independent, and standoffish like the Shiba. The commonalities they share are innate intelligence and a desire to work.

In coat type, the Shiba Retriever is most likely to have a coat that is medium in length, and that is composed of soft, silky hair. The ears may be prick eared like the Shiba's or floppy like those of the Golden. Coat colors range from cream to Irish Setter red to black and tan.

The Shiba Retriever's size varies dramatically with some dogs weighing 25 lbs (11 kg) and others 75 lbs (34 kg).

Corgi Inu

The cross breeding of a Shiba Inu and Pembroke Welsh Corgi is referred to as a Corgi Inu. Both dogs share in common a resemblance to a fox and have similar coat colors and ears. However, though these two breeds share similarities in looks with the exception of the length of the Corgi's body and its short legs, they bear little resemblance to one another in personality.

The ideal blending of these two dogs should produce a highly intelligent dog with fun loving personality. Corgis naturally enjoy the presence of their people while the Shiba is known for being independent of spirit, often preferring its own company.

In combining these two beloved breeds, the hope is to produce puppies that are more amenable to the process and more people driven.

Because this hybrid is in its infancy stages, it is not possible to determine what can be expected in terms of heights and weights. This will come in time.

Shepherd Inus

The resulting puppies of a German Shepherd bred to a Shiba Inu are referred to as Shepherd Inus. This dog breed is known for its exuberance and bold nature. A high energy breed, the Shepherd Inus needs regular exercise, and if possible, a job to do.

The Shepherd Inu can be extremely territorial. For this reason, they need early socialization and training to understand their boundaries to prevent the development of aggression.

In general, the Shepherd Inu is a breed of immense courage and loyalty that prefers the company of its family. However, the

Shiba aspect of this personality means this hybrid still highly prizes independence and is not known to be overly affectionate.

The Shepherd Inu retains the high prey drive of the Shiba. Obedience training is a must for this breed.

In appearance, the Shepherd Inu most closely resembles a wolf. Since both purebred breeds share similar ear types, their resulting offspring can be expected to have similar ear shape and carriage as well.

Coat colors can be any variation of the two breeds represented including red, black and tan, cream, or sesame. As is typical with both breeds, the Shepherd Inu will blow its coat twice yearly.

In size, the Shepherd Inu can reach up to 40-60 pounds (18-27 kg).

CHAPTER 16

Senior Shiba Inus

Shiba Inus enjoy a great life expectancy with the average being between 13 and 16 years. Still, Shibas do age, and when they enter their golden years, there is a period of adjustment to be made to help your Shiba to continue to enjoy excellent health.

Shiba Inus are considered seniors around age 10.

The senior years with your Shiba are especially special.

What Changes in Diet and Nutrition Will My Shiba Inu Experience?

To keep your senior Shiba Inu in optimal health, you will need to change its food to something that is better suited to the needs of elderly dogs. As a dog ages, they are no longer able to digest food as they once did. Since their activity requirements are fewer, their metabolism also begins to slow, making them more prone to retaining weight. The diet that was perfect for your Shiba in its youth must now be changed to accommodate the need associated with your dog's aging process.

If your dog has been on an adult formulation, it is now time to consider a move to a senior's food. Senior food is lower in protein to make it more easily digestible for your dog. The protein sources found in senior food are often obtained from blander sources such as white fish and chicken to make them easier for your elderly dog to process.

Senior foods also often contain smaller pieces of kibble. In their senior years, dogs often experience some dental decay, leaving their teeth less strong than they were in the prime of their live. Smaller pieces of food are easier for your Shiba to chew and require less force to break apart.

Some dogs begin to experience gum disease, making their mouths uncomfortable. If your Shiba falls into this category, canned food might be a viable option for them. Your veterinarian can provide you with some excellent suggestions as to how to best meet your senior dog's nutritional needs while easing any discomfort for its mouth.

What Changes Will Occur in My Shiba Inu's Drinking Habits and Bowel and Bladder Functions?

When dogs begin to age, their organs no longer function at peak capacity. Some of the more common medical problems your dog might experience include compromised kidney and liver function. Diabetes may also develop in some dogs. All of these ailments will increase your dog's desire to take in lots of fluids. If you notice your Shiba is drinking with more and more frequency, it is wise to make a visit to your vet to conduct regular geriatric testing, so you have a better understanding of how your dog's internal organs are functioning.

If your dog is experiencing a greater desire to drink water, this will be coupled with an increased need for bathroom breaks. Providing regular access to the outdoors is vitally important to your senior dog at this time.

Much like with Shiba puppies, your senior Shiba will start to lose its ability to control its bladder. This may mean that your dog begins to have accidents in the home. You can combat this problem by leaving puppy pee pads in areas of the house where your dog can go to relieve itself if it cannot hold its urine any longer. This will allow your senior dog to maintain some dignity and will cut down on the amount of mess that you need to clean.

As your Shiba ages, you will begin to notice changes in them. Regular veterinary care is important to keep them pain-free in the senior years.

What Do I Need to Know About Joint Pain and Stiffness in the Shiba Inu?

Most senior dogs of any breed will begin to suffer with arthritis as they age. Since Shiba Inus are a breed that enjoys being active, your first hint that your dog is suffering from arthritis often comes when your dog's pace an activity level begins to slow. You may notice that jumping on and off furniture takes longer and seems to elicit pain.

Joint pain and stiff muscles are very common in aging Shibas. Even if your elderly dog is not exhibiting any of the normal signs of pain, it is important to remember that dogs are masters at hiding discomfort. Your dog may be feeling extremely sore without your knowledge. Your veterinarian can help you assess your dog's body condition and if it is time to provide your dog with daily pain relief in the form of medication. Natural treatments such as heating pads and acupuncture can also prove effective treatments of suffering due to arthritis.

What Do I Need to Know About Vision and Hearing Problems in the Shiba Dog?

As your Shiba ages, it will begin to experience a decline in its vision and its hearing. Loss of these important senses dramatically impact your dog's quality of life. However, there are things you can do to assist your Shiba Inu with transitioning to its new way of life with duller senses.

To begin this process, it is wise to visit your veterinarian for a complete wellness examination. Your vet will be able to determine if your dog is currently undergoing hearing or vision loss and how advanced the condition is. At times, there will be measure that can be put in place to help slow the progression of any impairment.

If your dog is starting to go blind, you will notice them bumping into things more frequently. Since their confidence begins to wane with the loss of their vision, you will also find your dog wants to be close to you as often as possible. Your presence is a great comfort to a dog that is undergoing physical changes that are frustrating and scary.

Shiba Inus remain loyal and affectionate in their senior years.

What Do I Need to Know About Memory Loss and Confusion in Shiba Inus?

Canine cognitive dysfunction is a form of canine dementia. When a dog begins down this road, its memory is impaired, and the dog can become confused very easily. If you notice your dog wandering into corners and being unable to find its way out, dementia is likely to blame. There are some medications your veterinarian can prescribe which can help your dog to cope with the complications which result from confusion and disorientation as a result of canine cognitive dysfunction.

What Do I Need to Know About Changing Personality and Disposition in Shiba Inus?

Changes of personality can often occur during the senior years. Dogs that were once vibrant and energetic became much more sedate. Your Shiba that once so highly prized its independence may now become your constant shadow, craving both your presence and your affection.

You may also discover that your once gentle-natured Shiba Inu now will snap at people or other pets that encroach on its space while the dog is trying to rest. This is to be expected. Since your senior Shiba likely copes with at least some pain on a daily basis, being jostled around hurts, and your dog will respond in a fashion that will help prevent them from being injured as a result of overexuberant pets or family members who don't watch where they sit.

At some point, your Shiba will begin to descend into a mental state which is similar to depression. It is at this time that you must carefully evaluate your Shiba's quality of life to determine if it is time for you to help your beloved dog pass from this life to the next. The decision can only be made by you with the advice and support of your veterinarian. Though a very difficult choice to make; when your Shiba's quality of life has greatly deterioriated, this is sometimes the kindest thing that you can do for your most faithful friend.

When facing the senior years, it is important to remember that your dog has been your faithful friend for the entirety of its life. As time marches on, your dog deserves all of the comforts of a well-earned retirement.

CHAPTER 17
Conclusion

The Shiba Inu, the national treasure of Japan, is a special dog. Tracing its roots back to the ancient Asian Gray Wolf, this much-loved dog breed has strayed very little from its origins. A dog breed considered to be one of the oldest, the Shiba Inu's history goes back to 300 B.C where it was happily employed as a hunting companion for its beloved master. Over the years, the Shiba enjoyed many jobs including as a guardian of the home and a fighting dog. Today, this noble and stoic breed takes pride of place as a beloved family companion and continues to gain popularity in the United States, Canada, and around the world.

An independent thinker, the Shiba Inu is a naturally born problem solver. With the right amount of mental stimulation and exercise, the Shiba is a loyal companion that is happy to provide protection and affection for its cherished family members. A dog breed that can be prone to dog aggression, early socialization with socially appropriate dogs can help to combat this potential problem.

The Shiba Inu is known to be patient with children. However, supervision of all activities which involve children, and this breed, is a must.

A breed that is highly prized for its great intelligence, the Shiba excels when given a job to do. Though the breed's stubbornness can make training a challenge, your efforts will be richly rewarded. A versatile dog breed, the Shiba is equally at home in the show ring, in a variety of dog performance sports, or simply up on the couch beside you.

A dog with a bold, courageous nature, the Shiba's natural prey drive makes him well suited to hunting. This drive also translates to a friendly nature though the Shiba is naturally wary of strangers and takes time to warm to them.

Not necessarily a dog breed for the first-time owner; with the right amount of study and hard work, the Shiba can fit well into any home. The Shiba's activity requirements are modest, but the dog possesses immense stamina and endurance due to its early years traversing the mountainous terrain in its native Japan.

The Shiba Inu enjoys good health and an excellent longevity, living between 13-16 years. The most common inherited genetic diseases seen in Shiba Inus include hip and elbow dysplasia as well as eye disorders such as glaucoma.

Shiba Inus are a special breed!

Shibas enjoy excellent quality of life even into their senior years. With love, regular veterinary care, and proper nutrition, your beloved Shiba will be by your side for many years to come.

One thing is for certain; if a Shiba Inu has captured your heart, no other breed will do. When it comes to adding a Shiba to your home, you will find they are just like potato chips—it's impossible to stop at just one!

BONUS CHAPTER

Shiba Inu for Sale and Adoption

This bonus chapter focuses on providing you with the information you need to find a reputable Shiba Inu breeder or rescue organization in your area. Though this list is not exhaustive, it gives you an excellent starting point for your research. Many of the breeders or rescue organization can help you to network to find the right Shiba to add to your home.

Thank you for taking the time to read this book. We wish you great success in your search for your Shiba puppy. Great adventures await you with your new canine pal!

Shiba Inu Breeders in the United States

- **Sho Mai Sou (Victory Dancing Kennels)**
  http://www.shomaisou.com
  Ohio

- **Kari-On Shibas**
  http://www.kari-onshibas.com
  Arizona
- **Roki Yama Shibas**
  http://www.rokiyamashibas.com
  Colorado
- **Royal Kennels**
  http://www.royalkennels.com
  Ohio
- **Blue Door Kennel/Irezumi Shiba Inusv**
  http://thebluedoortattoo.com/blue-door-kennel/
  Colorado
- **Betty Rarick**
  http://kbarshibas.com
  Oklahoma
- **Goldkress Shibas**
  http://www.goldkressshibas.com
  Kansas
- **Showboat Kennels**
  http://www.showboatkennels.com
  Georgia
- **Monark Puppies**
  http://www.monarkpuppies.com
  Montana

- **Kenya Addington**
  http://kyscreeksidepuppies.com
  Montana
- **Sharon Krotzer**
  http://www.bestakcpups.com
  Minnesota

Shiba Inu Breeders in Canada

- **Shibachow Kennels**
  http://www.shibachow.com
  Quebec
- **SunoJo**
  http://www.sunojo.com/
  British Columbia
- **Satika Kennels**
  http://satika.ca/
  Alberta
- **Timberfox Kennels**
  http://timberfoxshibainu.com/
  Alberta
- **Koyote Kennels**
  http://www.calgaryshibas.com/
  Alberta

- **Driftwood Ranch**
  http://www.driftwoodranch.com/
  Alberta

Shiba Inu Breeders in the U.K.

- **Celtic Star Kennels**
  https://www.celticstarkennels.com/japanese-shiba-inu-gallery/
  Cwmann, Lampeter, Carmarthenshire
- **Marilouvales Japanese Shiba Inus**
  http://www.japaneseshibainu.co.uk/
  North Lincolnshire

Shiba Inu Rescue Groups in the United States

- **Midwest Shiba Inu Rescue**
  https://www.shibarescue.org/
  The Midwestern States of Minnesota, Nebraska, Iowa, Missouri, Kansas, Wisconsin, Michigan, Illinois, and Indiana
- **DC Shiba Rescue (DC SIR)**
  https://dcsir.org/
  Washington
- **Colorado Shiba Inu Rescue**
  http://coloradoshibainurescue.org/
  Colorado
- **Shiba Inu Rescue Organization**
  https://www.savingshibas.com/index.html
  Midwest

- **Central Florida Shiba Inu Rescue**
  https://savearescue.org/orgsandrescues/listing/central-florida-shiba-inu-rescue
  Florida
- **Shiba Inu Rescue Resources of America**
  http://sirra.shibas.org/
  Pennsylvania

Shiba Inu Rescue Groups in Canada

- **Greater Toronto Area Shiba Rescue**
  https://www.shibarescuegta.com/
  Ontario
- **National Shiba Inu Rescue**
  http://nationalshibarescue.org/ueme.org/ca
  Pacific Northwest
- **Petfinder**
  https://www.petfinder.com/dog-breeds/shiba-inu/
  Online resource

Shiba Inu Rescue Groups in the U.K.

- **Japanese Shiba Inu Rescue UK**
  http://www.japaneseshibainurescue.co.uk/
  Multiple locations

www.ingramcontent.com/pod-product-compliance
Lightning Source LLC
Chambersburg PA
CBHW070458100426
42743CB00010B/1674